OCCASIONAL PAPERS IN INTERNATIONAL AFFAIRS

Number 14

November 1966

THE ROLE OF THE MILITARY IN RECENT TURKISH POLITICS

By Ergun Özbudun

Published by the
Center for International Affairs
Harvard University

ABOUT THE AUTHOR

Dr. Ergun Özbudun, Assistant Professor of Government at the University of Ankara, spent the academic years 1963–66 at Harvard University under a Rockefeller Foundation fellowship which permitted him to undertake comparative research on political development and political parties. During much of his stay at Harvard he was associated with the Center for International Affairs, where he wrote the present paper. He is currently working on a study of the "pluralization" of single-party systems in Turkey and Mexico.

CONTENTS

Introduction*

On May 27, 1960, the Turkish Army overthrew the ostensibly strong and stable Menderes government, and thus put an end to the ten-year-old Democratic Party (DP) rule. The National Unity Committee (NUC), composed entirely of revolutionary officers, ruled the country until October, 1961, when it relinquished power to a freely elected civilian government. The 1960 coup was a turning point in recent Turkish history. Although many of the problems that plagued the First Turkish Republic remained unsolved during the NUC period or reasserted themselves after the return to civilian rule, political changes brought about by the coup were by no means negligible.

Not the least important of these changes was the adoption of a new Constitution and a new electoral system based on proportional representation. The Constitution of 1961, with its liberal provisions on civil liberties and its new legal-political institutions such as the upper chamber (Senate of the Republic), the Constitutional Court, the Supreme Council of Judiciary, and the State Planning Organization, was certainly not without effects on the political process. The impact of the eventful years of 1960–61 was also felt on the party system. At least two of the six parties represented in the present National Assembly can be considered the creations of the post-revolutionary period.[1] For the first time in Turkish history, an avowedly Socialist party, the Turkish Workers' Party (TWP), was able to operate freely and to win seats in the National Assembly. It should also be pointed out that the two-party system of the 1950s turned into a genuine multi-party system in the First Assembly (1961–65) of the Second Republic. Although the Justice Party

* I wish to acknowledge my great indebtedness to the Center for International Affairs for services rendered during the preparation of this monograph, as well as to the Rockefeller Foundation, whose support made the study possible. I am especially grateful to Professors Samuel P. Huntington, Rupert Emerson, and Richard D. Robinson (all of Harvard) and Professor Frederick W. Frey (of M.I.T.) for their valuable comments and suggestions.

[1]

(JP) won an absolute majority of seats in the National Assembly elections of 1965, it is still too early to speak about a return to the old two-party system. On the contrary, if proportional representation remains in effect, minor parties may be expected to retain and increase their representation at the expense of either one or both of the major parties.[2]

The principal political issues of the 1960s are also considerably different from those of the First Republic. The battle cries of Turkish politics in the 1950s revolved around constitutional problems and civil liberties. Despite the obvious bitterness of partisan struggle, the two major parties were not drawn apart by distinct social and political ideologies. On the contrary, their basic views on economic, social, and foreign policy were essentially similar, if not identical. On the classical left-right spectrum they could best be described as right-of-center parties. Since the 1960 Revolution, however, social and economic questions have increasingly come to the fore. The basic political cleavage now appears to be between a business liberalism and a reform-oriented statism. Foreign policy, which also remained virtually outside the realm of partisan conflict before 1960, has also tended to become a political issue.

It is clear that the 1960 coup provides an exceptionally good vantage point from which to study current Turkish politics. The subject should also be of considerable interest to students of comparative politics and of political development. In particular, the military intervention in Turkey dramatically illustrates the enormous difficulty of creating a stable democratic polity in a developing society. In fact, Turkey has been regarded by many observers as one of the very few non-Western countries capable of combining rapid modernization with democracy. As Frey has pointed out: "If Turkey, with her many advantages of able leadership, discipline, and capacity for self-sacrifice, could not work out these problems, what other emerging nation can do so?"[3] Thus, the tragic impasse to which Turkey has apparently come may be an omen of similar problems to be faced by other nations which have not yet reached the same stage of political development. It is hoped, therefore, that a study of the 1960 Turkish Revolution may shed some light on certain aspects of the process of political development, and particularly on the role of the military in this process.

The first empirical question to which I shall address myself is concerned with the conditions under which military interventions occur. To be sure, a good deal of ink has been spilled over this question; however, the circumstances that pulled the Turkish Army into the vortex of politics were considerably different from those in many other developing nations. The exceptional nature of the Turkish coup derives from the strength of the civilian political institutions in Turkey and from the tradition of a neutral army. Such a case should be clearly distinguished from the coups in which the military move into a power vacuum, unhampered by any tradition of civilian supremacy. Thus, the Turkish experience suggests that military interventions are not peculiar to the early stages of political development.

The second question is related to the function of the military coup with respect to social and economic change. Much has been said about the inherent conservatism of the professional military ethic and the tendency of military governments to maintain the status quo. Empirical evidence, as will be shown below, seems to support this argument. While the military support or initiate radical social reforms in a number of developing countries, such military leftism appears to be an exception rather than the rule. Furthermore, it is argued that even these progressive military regimes are not generally capable of providing effective economic leadership to a rapidly developing nation. Again, the Turkish coup is distinctive on both scores. It was an unquestionably reformist coup whose accomplishments in the field of economic development can hardly be minimized.

The basis for military leftism is another related question to which the Turkish experience may suggest an answer. While it may be wrong to explain the policy orientations of the military by any single factor, a close and logical correspondence can be observed between the political perspectives and the social background characteristics of the Turkish Army. It may be hypothesized that armies recruited essentially from lower or middle classes are more likely to produce reformist military regimes than armies of feudal or upper-class origins.

Finally, the dynamics of the Turkish coup should also be of interest to students of comparative military politics. The timing and the structure of the coup of May 27 conformed to what appears to be a more or less universal pattern. The familiar opposition between the military radicals and the moderates was also vividly felt within the Turkish Army. However, this conflict has

[3]

ended, for the time being at least, with the victory of the moderates, thus again distinguishing the Turkish case from most other military take-overs.

These distinctive characteristics have rendered the study of the Turkish coup of 1960 particularly useful for comparative purposes. In the pages that follow, I shall examine its causes, accomplishments, and dynamics with reference to the problems outlined above. It should be noted that the present paper is not intended to be either a comparative study of military coups or a general account of recent Turkish politics. Rather, its main concern is to test some hypotheses concerning the role of the military in developing countries against the Turkish experience. However, I felt it was necessary to compromise on both points. Thus, while some comparisons have been made with other countries to bring out the exceptional features of the Turkish coup, some elements of the Turkish political system other than the military have also been dealt with, for it is clear that the occurrence of a successful coup is not primarily related to the internal characteristics of the military forces but pertains to the functioning of the political system as a whole.[4]

I

The Political System and the Military: Conditions of Military Intervention

As pointed out, military intervention should be viewed primarily as a function of the total political system. Generally speaking, there is an inverse correlation between the frequency of successful coups and the strength of civilian political institutions, which, in turn, may be measured by such criteria as adaptability, complexity, autonomy, and coherence.[5] The existence of at least one strong, well-organized political party seems to be the best guarantee of civilian supremacy. Furthermore, "in modernizing systems, party institutionalization usually varies inversely with party competitiveness." Thus, it has been empirically demonstrated that military coups are more likely to occur in no-party or multi-party systems than in single-party, dominant single-party, or two-party regimes.[6]

The frequency of military intervention in politics is also determined by the nature of political culture, and especially by the strength of the tradition of civilian supremacy. Finer has distinguished four types or levels of political culture in terms of their proneness to military intervention. In countries with "mature political culture" legitimacy is paramount and unobtainable by the military. In countries with "developed political culture" legitimacy is important and resistive to military intervention. In countries with "low political culture" legitimacy is of some importance but is fluid. Finally, in countries with "minimal political culture" legitimacy is unimportant, and therefore resistance to military intervention is altogether negligible.[7]

Certainly, the level of political culture and the strength of the tradition of civilian supremacy vary with a number of factors. One way of achieving civilian control of the military is by

[5]

maximizing military professionalism. The professional military ethic requires the military officer to remain politically neutral. "A highly professional officer corps stands ready to carry out the wishes of any civilian group which secures legitimate authority within the state." The military man "is judged not by the policies he implements, but rather by the promptness and efficiency with which he carries them out. His goal is to perfect an instrument of obedience; the uses to which that instrument is put are beyond his responsibility."[8] Thus, the capacity of the military to intervene in politics is, in this sense, determined by the degree of military professionalism. The more highly professionalized an army is, the less likely it is to become involved in politics.

The distinctiveness of the Turkish coup can easily be seen against this comparative background. The intervention of the Turkish Army in politics can be attributed neither to the low level of political institutionalization nor to the lack of military professionalism. In fact, the First Turkish Republic, having achieved a balance between a relatively high degree of political institutionalization and a moderate rate of social mobilization, did not face the well-known problems of many modernizing systems. More specifically, Turkish political parties are among the best organized in the underdeveloped world, with highly centralized, disciplined, and cohesive organizations penetrating approximately three-fifths of the Turkish villages. "Turkish politics," as Frey said, "are party politics. . . . It is perhaps in this respect above all—the existence of extensive, powerful, highly organized, grass roots parties—that Turkey differs institutionally from the other Middle Eastern nations with whom we frequently compare her."[9] Thus, it is clear that the Turkish Army, unlike the armies in many other developing countries, did not move into a power vacuum which might have been created by the multiplicity, fluidity, and incoherence of political groups.

The level of political institutionalization can also be judged by the adaptability of a political organization or procedure. Adaptability, in turn, "is a function of environmental challenge and age. The more challenges which have arisen in its environment and the greater its age, the more adaptable it is."[10] By these criteria, too, both major Turkish political parties appear to be highly institutionalized. The People's Republican Party (PRP), for instance, successfully surmounted the problem of peaceful succession at the death of Atatürk in 1938. It survived a still more serious challenge when it transformed itself from a single-party to a pluralist party and then shifted from being the party in power to the party in opposition. The rarity of this type of transition is an indication of its difficulty. Indeed, few if any single-parties would have overcome such a crisis. The DP proved its own impressive institutional strength by its quick and complete recovery from the shock of the Revolution of 1960: only a year and a half afterwards, the Justice Party, the successor of the DP, was a major partner in the coalition government, and in October 1965, it was once again the governing party of Turkey with a popular majority of 53 per cent. One hardly needs to emphasize that any party that could survive a successful military coup against it owes a great deal to the strength and adaptability of its organization.

It should also be noted that the rates of social mobilization and political participation in Turkey were not very high in the 1950s. It may be true that the peasants—until this time largely apathetic and indifferent—began to acquire a "rudimentary sense of citizenship" as well as a limited opportunity to participate in politics.[11] Nevertheless, this increased participation did not seem to result in a loss of autonomy and coherence on the part of political institutions and in their subordination to outside influences.[12] On the contrary, the center of gravity of Turkish politics remained essentially an intra-elite conflict. Or rather, we have witnessed "the resurrection of severe intra-elite conflict," which was resolved in the Kemalist era. Although the support of the peasantry was crucial for the Democrats, the leadership of the party remained firmly in the hands of commercial-legalistic urban elites. The rural masses, being poorly organized and still not fully conscious of their political potentialities, were not in a position to exert much pressure on the Democratic government, and, being out of sympathy with the PRP for a variety of reasons, they did not have much choice but to continue voting for the Democrats. The DP leadership was not, as it has sometimes been assumed, pushed into conflict with other elite groups as a result of the irresistible pressures of the villagers: it could afford to engage in a bitter and unrestrained intra-elite conflict because of its "insulating power base" in the rural areas.[13] In other words, while the availability of non-elites somewhat increased in the last two decades, the accessibility of elites still remained low.[14] "Participation explosion," the major source of political instability and institutional decay in many developing countries, was not a factor of prime importance in Turkey.

All this does not mean, of course, that the civilian political system in Turkey was functioning properly in the late 1950s. In fact, the very incidence of the coup indicates that such was not the case. A combination of various factors, but above all the virulent intra-elite conflict mentioned above, caused the civilian rule to break down. Still, this is substantially different from the cases in other countries in which either the inherent weakness or the subsequent deterioration of civilian political institutions made the military perhaps the only candidate to fill the power vacuum.

The Turkish coup of 1960 also differs from most military take-overs with respect to the second major precondition of military intervention in politics: the lack of military professionalism. It is safe to say that, despite an historical and cultural background which usually encourages military rule, the tradition of a neutral army and civilian supremacy had firmly taken root in Turkey, as evidenced by almost four decades of unbroken civilian rule. The gradual but decisive steps taken by Atatürk to ensure the depoliticization of the army have been examined in detail elsewhere, and need not be treated at length here.[15] It has been argued, however, that the separation of the military from politics was not complete: the civilian regime was dependent on the support of the army to maintain its power and to implement its reforms; former officers continued to be recruited into important political roles at the ministerial, parliamentary, and administrative levels; and the contentment of the armed forces with the nonpolitical roles they had been assigned may have been due to the fact that their ex-commanders were the leaders of the new regime and they were carrying out a social revolution which the army desired.[16] Granting these points, the First Turkish Republic was still very far from being a "praetorian state."[17] Civilian supremacy was clearly established and never challenged. The military played a relatively minor and steadily decreasing role in the determination of public policy. In short, the Turkish coup of 1960 suggests that even a highly professionalized army may find itself in a situation which makes military intervention almost inescapable.

What were the causes and the nature of this revolutionary situation in Turkey? How are we to explain the breakdown of a highly institutionalized civilian political system and the sudden thrust of a professional army into politics? The failure of the multi-party experiment in Turkey, of which the coup of 1960 is but one symptom, is certainly a momentous question to which there is no simple answer. Presented herein is a discussion of some of the more specific causes of the Turkish Revolution as pointed out by earlier students of the subject. To be sure, the coup of 1960 was the result of a combination of factors, and weighing the respective importance of each is, in part, a subjective task. Since these explanations greatly vary in factual accuracy and logical consistency, however, such a discussion may still be of use.

Lamentably, much of what has been written in Turkey on this subject is laden with emotion and therefore does not meet scholarly standards. For example, a Turkish scholar-turned-politician, Ali Fuad Basgil, cites the following factors as responsible for the Revolution: "the perfidious maneuvers of the opposition," "the disloyalty of certain intellectual circles," and the irresponsible exploitation by the press of the traditionally oppositional mentality of the Turkish people. While he concedes some errors by the Democrats, what he considers their "capital error" is their failure to recognize "the malice of passions of their adversaries."[18] Basgil does not explain, however, why the army was more susceptible to the appeal of the opposition than to that of the government, or why the Turkish press chose to side with the opposition despite heavy government pressure and considerable risks involved in criticizing the government.

No one can rightfully say that the coup was made on behalf of the major opposition party (PRP). The radical group in the NUC did not trust the PRP much more than it did the Democrats, and the rest of the Committee went out of its way to ensure the honesty of the 1961 elections. Although an early election might well have given the PRP a clear victory, elections were postponed until October 1961, thus giving the Justice Party and the New Turkey Party (NTP) full opportunity to organize the old Democratic electorate.

Nor is the argument to be taken seriously linking the coup to the personal animosity of General Gürsel caused by his disappointment in the matter of promotion to the top post in the army.[19] To be passed over for Chief of Staff, which is hardly a more prestigious position than commander of the land forces,

[9]

does not seem to be a sufficiently powerful motive to make a revolutionary out of a professional soldier, whose later acts, moreover, clearly showed his belief in a nonpolitical army. Furthermore, the 1960 coup was not essentially the work of one man. Gürsel was not one of the instigators of the conspiracy, and he played almost no role in the planning and execution of the coup. He was chosen to head the NUC because of the fear of the younger revolutionaries that they might not be able to command the loyalty of their superiors unless they worked under the leadership of a popular and highly respected general. Finally, even in power, Gürsel's influence on the NUC was very far from being absolute, and on a number of occasions he failed to carry a majority of the NUC with him.[20]

Another theory which deserves closer examination is based on the difference between the levels of modernity of the civilian and military institutions. It has been convincingly argued that, for a number of reasons, "modern armies are somewhat easier to create in transitional societies than are most other forms of modern social structures," and that the armies are therefore likely to be the most modernized organs in such societies.[21] Thus, if the civilian political institutions lag behind in modernizing themselves and the society, the military, being extremely sensitive to the needs of modernization and technological advancement, may feel a strong compulsion to take control.

There is little doubt about the general validity of this proposition. In the case of Turkey, for nearly two centuries the army has been more modern than the civilian institutions and is the foremost modernizer of the Turkish society. The Young Turks' revolution and Atatürk's military-based regime may, in fact, be largely explained by the failure of the civilian sector to match the modernity of the military establishment. But whether this was still true in the 1950s is open to question. Lerner and Robinson take pains to show that the civilian leadership under the PRP rule "diverted relatively little of its total effort to a revamping and modernizing of the military forces." Consequently, after World War II, the army

was no longer the *avant-garde* of modernization as it had been in Ottoman times. Nor was it now a channel of upward mobility around a frozen civilization elite. Civilians were clearly in a position of unchallenged supremacy, politically and technologically, and it was in the civilian hierarchy that ability was most clearly recog-

[10]

nized as a basis for promotion and power. . . . The military hierarchy froze and went into suspended animation; the civilian hierarchy opened up and led the way to innovation.[22]

Lerner and Robinson argue, however, that this situation radically changed after 1948 as a result of a two-sided development. On one hand the Turkish army, especially due to American military and technical aid, regained its position as a modern social institution and a crucial agent of modernization. On the other hand, channels of mobility were clogged in the civilian administration which became a "closed society" and could not match the army's dynamism.

It would appear, however, that both sides of this picture are somewhat exaggerated. While the influence of the military steadily declined in the single-party years, it was still much stronger than in the 1950s. It is also disputable whether ability was less rewarded in the army than in the civilian sector. Actually, the merit system was more strictly followed by the military than by the civilian hierarchy, even though advancement was slow.[23] In addition, what occurred between 1948 and 1960 does not appear to have had a force sufficient to reverse the respective positions of the civilian and military hierarchies on the scale of modernity. The contention that the military attracted large numbers of able and ambitious growth elements in the population as a consequence of the greater social mobility it offered in the 1950s does not agree with the facts. The military, as will be shown below, has always offered better avenues of advancement to the sons of lower and lower-middle classes. The appeal of the military profession to what is identified as the "growth elements" of the society—modern intellectuals, technicians, the innovators and entrepreneurs—has never been great during the history of the Republic and was even less so in the 1950s. In fact, if any trend could be established, it would in all probability indicate a marked decline in the prestige of the military profession. Engineering, law, medicine, commerce, and banking were the most sought-after careers during this period; few sons of middle-class families ever thought of the military as a career.[24] Finally, there is little evidence to show that channels of mobility in the civilian sector were clogged during the DP administration. On the contrary, despite the existence of partisan pressures, the encouragement of private enterprise must have opened new channels of advancement to the rising middle class from which

[11]

the Democrats drew their cadres. In short, the Turkish Army in 1960 was not appreciably more modern than Turkish civilian political institutions. It had neither a monopoly of technological skills nor a monopoly of social mobility. This does not mean, however, that the army did not have an image of modernization quite different from that of the DP leaders.

Another interesting attempt has been made to link the 1960 coup to the loss of power and prestige by the military under DP rule. "The . . . military action that extinguished the First Republic," argues Frey, "must in part be understood in terms of the sharp decline in representation and power of erstwhile military men in the Grand National Assembly and its cabinet."[25] As pointed out above, the recruitment of former military figures into important political roles was quite common in the Kemalist era. However, the representation of the military in the National Assembly and the cabinet gradually but steadily declined even in this period, and almost reached a vanishing point with the rise of the DP. Thus, the military contingent in the Assembly dwindled from about 15 or 20 per cent to a mere 4 per cent in the Tenth Assembly (1954–57). Similarly, the percentage of cabinet ministers with military background fell from about 30 or 35 per cent to 15 per cent in the Eighth Assembly (1946–50), the last Assembly with a PRP majority, and there was not a single military figure in the cabinets of the Tenth Assembly.[26]

This change, however, was to be expected. The military profession does not normally provide its members with such appropriate political skills as bargaining, compromise, negotiation, and persuasion.[27] It is understandable, therefore, that in "developed" political systems, democratic or otherwise, the political power of the military is low, and few political leaders come from the military profession. A Western parliamentary democracy seems to give disproportionate influence to "specialists in persuasion" and in particular to the legal profession.[28] To be sure, the situation may be radically different in a transitional society. An army-based tutelary regime, for example, naturally tends to give a large share of power to the military at its formal levels of authority. But even in this case, the representation of the military is likely to decline with the consolidation of the revolutionary regime and the return to normality. This is precisely what happened in two model tutelary regimes, both of which were heavily dependent on the military in the early stages of their development: Turkey and

Mexico. The crucial factor in this process seems to be the pattern of policy of the civilian regime rather than the composition of the political elite. The Turkish and Mexican experiences suggest that so long as the civilian government continues to carry out programs cherished by the military, the latter are not likely to become disaffected by their loss of formal power. In fact, as Frey has shown, the representation of the military in government dwindled in the Kemalist era without weakening the foundations of the civilian authority. The discontent of the Turkish Army with the DP government should, therefore, be explained not essentially in terms of the decline of military political power but in terms of the governmental policies with which the Turkish military strongly disagreed.[29] These policies can be categorized as follows: (1) increasing authoritarianism, (2) ambivalence toward modernity and secularism, and (3) ultra-conservative social and economic policies.

Many students of the Turkish Revolution stress that the repressive policies of the Menderes government against the opposition and the unconstitutional laws which restricted civil liberties to an extent unprecedented in the multi-party period were the main sources of resentment among officers as well as intellectuals.[30] It is true that the last years of the Democratic administration were filled with constitutional crisis, and there can be no doubt about the unconstitutionality of the law establishing "the Committee to Investigate the Activities of the Republican People's Party and a Section of the Press" which set in motion the rioting and persecution that immediately preceded the fall of the regime.[31] A good deal of evidence suggests that these incidents increased the hostility of the military against the Menderes regime. For example, on May 3, 1960, General Gursel sent a letter to the government through the Defense Minister protesting police brutalities against students, demanding the repeal of antidemocratic laws, the abolition of the Investigating Committee, the release of journalists and students arrested in connection with the recent incidents, and the resignation of President Bayar.[32] Many members of the NUC, in press interviews after the Revolution, clearly expressed their resentment against the repressive measures taken by the Menderes government, and stated that they felt compelled to stage a coup in order to save the nation from an increasingly authoritarian regime.[33] Furthermore, the declaration prepared by a group of law professors in the name of the NUC

[13]

justified the coup completely on the ground that the DP administration had lost its legitimacy because of its unconstitutional acts.[34]

Similar views can be expressed about the resentment aroused by the use of the armed forces for police purposes during the last months of the Democratic administration. The reluctance of the military to get involved in police functions is understandable from a professional point of view. "The military," Janowitz argues, "either as a result of the influence of Western forms or because of self-generated heroic ideals, seeks, wherever possible, to withdraw from the continuous task of day-to-day policing and repression of political opposition. . . . It seems to operate on the assumption that minor day-to-day resort to force weakens its organizational capacity to intervene successfully with shock tactics and with overpowering impact. This appears to be an application of the military theme of conservation of resources."[35] It can also be said that if the legality and basic morality of such repressions are questionable, as in the Turkish case, the military man is not likely to feel himself bound by the imperatives of the professional military ethic, which normally exalts obedience as his highest virtue.[36] As the Democrats attempted to use the army to suppress the PRP, thus willy-nilly involving the army in politics, they destroyed the last barrier to military intervention: the neutral army tradition.[37]

While this explanation is basically sound, it leaves some points open to question. It is not clear, for example, whether the Turkish military was categorically against any kind of authoritarianism and totally committed to parliamentary democracy at all costs, or was only against a right-wing authoritarianism as typified by the Menderes regime. It should be noted that the military was the main pillar of the reformist but unquestionably authoritarian Kemalist rule. Certainly, the conditions which existed when the foundations of the Kemalist regime were laid were vastly different from those in the 1950s. But even in the 1920s Turkey had already had some experience in multi-party politics, and the Progressive Party opposition of 1924–25, interestingly enough led by some prominent military figures, strongly advocated a parliamentary democracy. Still, the bulk of the Turkish military chose to side with Atatürk and to pursue a path of authoritarian reform. There was some unrest in the army in the last years of the PRP rule, and after 1946 secret military groups

[14]

were formed with the intention of preventing another rigged election.[38] However, not all officers viewed the Democrats' electoral victory in 1950 favorably. Even after the decisive showing of the DP, some senior generals approached Inönü to sound out his attitude toward military intervention. They were categorically rebuffed.[39]

This ambivalent attitude of the Turkish military toward multi-party parliamentarianism also manifested itself in the NUC period. A strong faction of the Committee, perhaps even a majority of its members, was more concerned with basic social reforms than an early return to a constitutional regime. It appears that only an unusual combination of circumstances prevented this group from gaining the upper hand. It should also be noted that the planning of the coup had begun long before the previous constitutional crisis and the brutal repression of opposition and student activities. Finally, the attempted coups of 1962 and 1963 obviously had nothing to do with the authoritarianism of the civilian coalition governments. The conflict within the NUC and the Turkish Army over the question of civilian rule will be examined below in more detail. It suffices to say here that not all members of the military group that seized power in 1960 acted from the same motives. For some, the main purpose of the coup was to put an end to a repressive regime and to set the nation back on a democratic road; for others, the coup was intended to be a continuation of the Atatürk Revolution, presumably through an extended period of military rule. But it can be safely argued that even for the military moderates the discontent with the DP regime did not derive solely from the authoritarian tendencies of the latter.

One of the most frequently heard charges against the DP regime was that the DP leaders betrayed the Atatürk Revolution. A few quotations from the interviews with the NUC members clearly show how widespread this feeling was in the revolutionary committee. General Gürsel: "I am convinced that the reforms retrogressed during the period now behind us. In fact this was the greatest evil." Colonel Türkes: "The Atatürk reforms did not mark time, they retrogressed. They retrogressed in the field of religion, of dress and, most importantly, of mentality." Colonel Köksal: ". . . He [Bayar] and his associates were not devoted to Atatürk. They didn't love him. I definitely obtained this impression from their acts and from their words." Major Erkanlı: They

[15]

[i.e., the DP leaders] sabotaged the primary education mobilization. They demeaned the 'One school for each village' campaign. They destroyed treasonably and for partisan reasons the People's Houses and the People's Rooms. They mercilessly extinguished nests of culture. By these actions they proved once more their hostility toward Atatürk and culture. . . . They encouraged the old [i.e., Arabic] script in order to blunt the desire of our youth to read and write." Captain Solmazer: "They [the Atatürk reforms] retrogressed a great deal. The reforms strayed from their basic routes. They were betrayed." Lieutenant Colonel Kabibay: "The 27 May Revolution was a rising-up of the present generation trained by the revolutionary spirit of Atatürk with a view to protecting and rescuing the revolution of the great Atatürk from those who, during the last ten years, wanted to upset and destroy it out of a thirst for power." Colonel Yurdakuler: "After 1950 I saw with regret that they [the DP leaders] were leaving the civilized road which Atatürk had outlined for the improvement of the Turkish nation, that the nation was being dragged backwards, that a rapid retrogression was commencing in every field. . . . It naturally could not continue."[40]

The attitude of the DP government toward Atatürk reforms and modernization can best be described as ambivalent. It is true that Menderes and his lieutenants actually neither wanted nor could afford a religious reaction which would endanger the foundations of the secular Republic. As Frey has summarized, "the Democratic Party, though willing to support a mild religious 'revival' (actually, a partial easing of previous restraints rather than a revival), was basically quite modern in its top personnel and quite committed in its own way to a continuation of modernization, even while trying to make political capital out of the religious issue."[41] It is implicit in this statement that the commitment of the DP to modernization "in its own way" was substantially different from the Kemalist model. Much has been written about the "revival of Islam" in Turkey in the 1950s, but this is too broad a question to discuss here.[42] Still, it should be noted that this period witnessed a reawakening of interest in religion; an uncontrolled flow of religious (and often reactionary) literature; a vast increase in the number of private Koran schools taught mostly by illiterate village *hocas;* the reappearance of reactionary sects and orders (such as *Ticanîler* and *Nurcular:* the former waged a systematic campaign of destruction against

[16]

statues and portraits of Atatürk, and the latter are believed to have considerable political influence); and a partial return to some traditional ways of life particularly in matters of the status, dress, and public demeanor of women.

It can be argued, of course, that a heightened interest in religion is perfectly compatible with secularism and modernization.[43] But, as the developments outlined above would indicate, the easing of previous restraints has "helped undermine the secularist spirit to the benefit of Islam, not the enlightened progressive Islam, but the same old obscurantist, fatalistic type which has dominated the Turkish masses since time immemorial."[44] Furthermore, it is to be remembered that secularism had a different and much more comprehensive meaning in Kemalist Turkey than in the West. Kemalist secularism did not limit itself to the separation of religious from political affairs. It also aimed at liberating "the society from the hold of Islam, and to bring about a new type of free individual. It was a rationalist, scientific-minded, anti-traditionalist, and anti-clericalist secularism." Therefore, the critics of Turkish secularism may be theoretically right in that "the old conception of the state subordinated to religion had been replaced by the conception of religion bound to the state, and both conceptions violated the principle of secularism."[45] However, given the fatalistic and obscurantist nature of the religious beliefs among the Turkish masses, a mere separation between the state and religion would certainly not be enough to create a modern society based on rational and scientific thinking. Alternatives open to the Kemalist cadres in the 1920s were either to reform Islam radically enough to become a progressive force, or to restrict religious liberties to a greater extent than in secular Western states. In view of the enormous difficulties involved in the first alternative, it was only natural that the latter course was chosen.

This special character of Turkish secularism helps us to understand the sensitivity of modern Kemalists to recent developments outlined above. Even though they are not opposed to Islam as a religion and do not generally believe that the religious revival of the 1950s would seriously endanger the foundations of the secular republican state, they are still deeply disturbed by the concessions made to religious conservatives and by the use of religious issues for political purposes. The attitude of the NUC toward Islam and secularism is typical of a great

[17]

majority of modern Kemalists. Although many of the Committee members are said to be practicing Muslims, and some have expressed a strong interest in encouraging an enlightened Islam, they all unequivocally condemned the exploitation of religion for political ends and the retrogression of Kemalist secularism in the multi-party period.[46]

Another important cause of the 1960 Turkish Revolution may be found in the DP administration's social and economic policies which received insufficient attention in earlier studies of the subject. Apart from rampant graft and corruption, which certainly clashed with the puritanical military ethic, these policies were essentially designed to serve the interests of such economically dominant groups as large landowners and businessmen. Frey has vividly shown the increased representation in the Grand National Assembly of traders and agriculturists with the accession of the Democrats. "Along with the provincial lawyer, the small-town merchant or tradesman seems to typify the changed Assemblies of the Democratic Party's decade of control, just as the official and the officer typified the Kemalist epoch."[47] Furthermore, the greatly increased contingent of lawyers was very likely to include a substantial proportion of persons with landed interests.

The domination of commercial-agricultural groups seemed to be even stronger on the local levels of the DP (and now the JP) hierarchy. Thus, Tachau has observed that 67 per cent of the members of provincial executive committees of the Justice Party in twelve selected provinces were traders and industrialists (as opposed to 38 per cent of the Republican local leaders). A more intensive study of the party organizations in two specific provinces (Adana and Aydin) also tended to confirm this observation.[48] A survey of local opinion leaders in the provinces of Eskisehir and Diyarbakır carried out by a Turkish political scientist, Nermin Abadan, yielded parallel results. The respondents estimated that over four-fifths of the peasants and close to one-half of the merchants and traders supported the JP.[49]

Finally, it should be noted that traders and agriculturists remained most loyal to the Democrats throughout the 1950s. While "the intellectual and professional support that had been given to the Democrats from 1946 on was significantly undermined by the repressions of the Menderes-Bayar government," there is little evidence of the alienation of the traders and farmers from the DP regime on the eve of the Revolution. "Curtailment of newly won democratic rights does not seem to have struck these vocational groups as being a fundamental political issue."[50]

Given the social composition of their party, it was natural that the Democratic leaders would give top priority to the interests of business and farming groups. Thus, during the decade of DP control, private enterprise flourished due to a policy of economic liberalism and enlarged credit facilities. The tax system put the main burden of public services on salaried personnel, while tax evasion in commerce and industry mounted to unusually high figures. In the field of industrial relations, Democrats continuously denied the workers the right to strike and the right of collective bargaining, despite the promises the party had made before taking power. Trade unions were kept under strict government control, and, quite naturally, they have made little progress under such unfavorable conditions.

Similarly, in the field of agriculture, policies favoring economically dominant groups were followed. In one sense the Democratic Party was born out of the opposition to the Land Reform of 1945, for the strongest criticism against the law was voiced by two deputies who were to be the future founders of the Democratic Party, Menderes and Koraltan.[51] While the distribution of government-owned land continued in the Democratic era, genuine land reform measures such as the distribution of large private estates were not even considered. It is illustrative that one of the very few back-bench rebellions in the DP parliamentary group occurred in 1955 when the government proposed a modest increase in the land tax. The government, which was almost always able to get its bills through the Assembly with the support of its obedient parliamentary majority, had to give way and withdraw its proposal.[52]

On the other hand, it must be admitted that not only the owners of large estates, but the bulk of the small farmers benefited, to a certain extent, from the agricultural subsidies, the rise of agricultural prices, the abolition of certain taxes on agriculture, and the lessening of government controls and pressures under the Democratic administration. A more dynamic, although hazardous, economic policy provided new jobs for millions of people. However, it is generally agreed that these agricultural policies "resulted in the improved welfare of only a small number

[19]

of landowners and neglected the population at large."[53] As an American economist has written:

Through 1953, the Turkish farm mechanization program had probably directly benefited only 25,000-27,500 (scarcely over 1 per cent) of Turkey's farm families. These few families probably enjoyed average annual gross cash incomes in excess of $15,000 each and were the recipient of at least 25 per cent of the public farm credit outstanding to all Turkish farmers at the end of 1952. . . . Turkey has tended to follow—first in industry, now in agriculture what I would call the "showcase" type of economic development. That is, at the expense of population at large, some small group of producers is heavily protected, subsidized and otherwise favorably treated to become a symbol of progress in which few of their fellow citizens can share. A few islands of privilege in a sea of poverty nonetheless are a poor indicator of economic development.[54]

Whatever may be said for or against the economic policies of the Democrats, it is clear that social justice was not a main consideration. On the whole, Turkey was certainly a more dynamic society in the 1950s than in the previous decades, but hardly a more balanced one. Differences of wealth seem to have increased, carrying with them the seeds of potentially greater social conflict.

There is ample evidence suggesting that the conservative economic policies of the Menderes regime and unbalanced distribution of income created a deep concern among the Turkish military. A few quotations from the statements of the NUC members illustrate this point. Major Erkanlı, one of the masterminds of the coup, asserted that the Democrats "dragged the country into disaster in the economic and social fields. . . . An unreasonable consumption began. In 10 years we became one of the poorest nations in the world. This and similar reasons prepared the platform of the 27 May revolution." He went on to say that the NUC regards "as illegal incomes which are not the return of physical and mental labor and which do not accord with the sense of social justice. . . . We hate the refrain, 'there are 15 millionaires in every quarter and 1,500 hungry people in every village.' I compare the national wealth to water in joint receptacles. A definite balance must be established between capital and labor. No one must be allowed to exploit another person. . . . Even a one-*kurus* [the 100th part of a Turkish *lira*] investment which does not aid our production is a crime. Waste must become our greatest enemy." Captain Özdag claimed that under the DP rule "our market was a colonial bazaar. . . . The development effort remained no more than an absurd fantasy." Lieutenant Colonel M. Kaplan argued that "the corruption in the country . . . and the social decay which was going on at great speed were veiled and concealed by a policy of greed based on group domination under the guise of economic development." It is highly significant that 19 out of 29 NUC members for whom we have interview data regarded social justice and/or land reform as one of the most important problems of the country.[55]

The discontent of the Turkish military with the economic policies of the Menderes regime can be explained by two factors. First, the military were among the groups which suffered most directly and visibly from the rampant inflation, the effects of which were by no means matched by the very modest increases in salaries. But even deeper sources of dissatisfaction can be sought in the social composition of the Turkish Army. It stands to reason that the Turkish military, being recruited largely from the lower-middle class, were extremely sensitive to policies favoring a small wealthy minority at the expense of social justice. The hypothesized relationship between the social backgrounds of the Turkish military and their policy orientations in social and economic fields will be examined in the next chapter at greater length. It should be noted, however, that to point to the relevance of economic grievances as a cause of the military intervention is far from saying that the 1960 coup was essentially a social revolution. The revolutionary officers did not have a distinct social philosophy apart from a somewhat vague social neo-Kemalism. Nevertheless, such an emphasis on economic factors may help in understanding the deep interest of the NUC in social reforms far more comprehensive than those advocated by the People's Party. In other words, only by assuming that a strong progressivist tendency existed among the Turkish officers, can we understand why the military regime of 1960–61, despite its avowedly transitional nature, became so involved in economic affairs. The next chapter gives an account of the economic and social reforms accomplished or attempted by the NUC.

II

Military Intervention and Social Change: Soldiers as Reformers

The political outlook of the military has often been identified as an essentially conservative one. Huntington has argued, for example, that "while inherent contrast and conflict exist between the military ethic and liberalism, fascism, and Marxism, inherent similarity and comparability exist between the military ethic and conservatism. . . . In its theories of man, society, and history, its recognition of the role of power in human relations, its acceptance of existing institutions, its limited goals, and its distrust of grand designs, conservatism is at one with the military ethic."[56] While this description fits well the military elite of Western countries, the position of the military in relation to social change varies greatly in developing societies. Thus, "the military has been a vigorous champion of progress and development in some countries and a retarding influence in others."[57]

But even when the military is a progressive force, its capacity to carry out far-reaching social reforms and to supply effective economic leadership to a rapidly developing nation is questioned by many students of military politics. It is argued, for example, that while the military may be able to secure more rational and orderly management of certain specific economic activities, they seem to manifest some basic limitations, inherent in the profession, in providing central economic direction and leadership.[58] Thus Shils has asserted that once the military rulers have succeeded in

suppressing attempted *putsches,* cleaning up streets, removing beggars from the center of the main towns, prosecuting the beneficiaries of the preceding regime, and preventing the spread of rumors of corruption about its own regime . . . there is not much more that they can do to support their own self-confidence and to impress themselves on the public mind. Since they have very little of a program except what they take over from the planning boards and civil servants of the old regime, for whom they have no respect, they are left directionless . . . so there is a danger that they will come to feel suspended in a void of clean government and clean streets.[59]

Generally speaking, three types of military coups can be distinguished: governmental coup (or "palace revolution"), revolutionary coup, and reform coup. The 1960 Turkish coup falls neatly into the last category. In fact, as is typical of reform coups, the revolutionary officers were "highly nationalistic, progressive, authoritarian, and developmental-minded." Although they did not "instigate a convulsive revolutionary process," they did make some reforms in the political, economic, and social structure.[60] The accomplishments of the NUC were certainly not confined to "cleaning up the government" and "cleaning up the streets."

One of the most important reforms accomplished by the NUC was the establishment of the State Planning Organization. Although economic planning had been advocated by the People's Party opposition in the 1950s, the military influence undoubtedly played a large part in the establishment of this organization and its inclusion in the Constitution.[61] Later events showed that the military and political parties had different views as to the role to be assigned to the planners. While the planners were given a relatively free hand within broadly defined economic goals during the NUC rule, they began to have an increasingly difficult time under the civilian governments. It may be assumed that many civilian politicians resented what they considered to be an encroachment upon their authority by a group of technocrats. Under these pressures and strains almost all top planning officials had to resign after 1961 and were replaced by seemingly more pliable and more conservative bureaucrats.

Another measure taken by the NUC was the inclusion of agricultural income as a taxable category. This, however, was to apply only to large and middle-sized farm operators. Significantly, the agricultural sector, which provides about three-fourths of the Turkish national income, has for many decades been exempt from an agricultural income tax. The efforts to correct this gross deficiency had always been successfully met by the resistance of landed interests through their influence on political parties. This influence was manifested once again when the civilian coalition government of Inönü lowered the tax rates

[23]

established by the NUC and further limited the field of application of the new tax law.

The revisions made by the NUC in land and building tax rates met a similar fate. These taxes, based on assessments made decades ago, had become insignificant as a consequence of inflation and the rising value of land and buildings. When the NUC decided to increase these taxes between five and ten times the 1942 level, it became the target of criticism by parties and powerful interest groups. Interestingly, one of the few conflicts between the NUC and the Constituent Assembly, in which the People's Party had an overwhelming majority, concerned the rates of land and building taxes. Eventually, under the pressure of the civilian politicians and landowners, the NUC had to cut the proposed tax increases.

If this was one of the occasions of friction between the military and the civilian political forces, another such conflict centered on a similar problem—namely, the constitutional provision on land reform. Article 38 of the present Turkish Constitution states that:

> The State and other corporate bodies, where public interest deems it necessary, are authorized, subject to the principles and procedures as set forth in the pertinent law, to expropriate the whole or a part of any immovable property under private ownership, or to impose an administrative servitude thereon provided that the true equivalent value is immediately paid in cash.
>
> The form of payment of the true equivalent values of land expropriated for the purpose of enabling farmers to own land, for nationalization of forests, for afforestation, and for accomplishing the establishment of settlement projects shall be provided by law. Where the law deems it necessary that payment be made by installments, the period of payment shall not exceed ten years. In this event, the installments shall be paid in equal amounts and shall be subject to interest rates prescribed by law.

This provision, particularly the ten-year period of payment in installments, created a storm in the House of Representatives of the Constituent Assembly. During the debates Article 38 was severely criticized by the right-wing of the People's Party, and the period in question was cut to five years by the House. On the insistence of the NUC on a ten-year period, however, the House had to give way, and the original provision was retained. It is interesting to note that no serious steps have been taken towards its implementation since 1961. One of the reasons of the fall of the third Inönü government is said to have been the moderate land reform bill it finally submitted to the National Assembly.

Another measure of the NUC on the economic and financial front was the inauguration of the Declaration of Wealth. This measure was designed to prevent the unusually high degree of tax evasion. As in the case of other social reforms attempted by the Committee, the outcry from the parties and the business groups was immediate. At the end, the Inönü government returned the declarations to be filled out anew; but the business groups, apparently not satisfied with this move, continued to lobby for the outright repeal of the Declaration of Wealth.

Finally, the NUC decided to remove fifty-five *agas* (owners of large lands and often of many villages) to compulsory residence in western Turkey and to confiscate their lands for future distribution, with the hope of breaking the semi-feudal system predominant in many parts of eastern Turkey. Interestingly, one of the first actions of the PRP-JP coalition government which followed the NUC rule was to return the *agas* to their places and to restore all their land and property that had not yet been distributed.[62]

What is the final balance sheet for the economic and social reform of the NUC? Weiker is correct in observing that the NUC experience did not result "in important changes which might work to prevent a recurrence of the situation that preceded the NUC," and that "a large part of the cause of the NUC's failure to achieve more in relation to these problems lay in its failure to exploit its political position. . . . In acting more like orthodox politicians—and politicians with only minority support—than like nonpolitical, problem-solving soldiers, the NUC may have missed what was a unique opportunity for Turkey to return to the road of rapid development."[63] The basic dilemma that plagued the NUC and explains its failure to exploit fully its political position was the contradiction between its two goals: to carry out basic social reforms, and to return power to a democratically elected civilian government as early as possible. Given the NUC commitment to the latter goal, it is difficult to see how they could have avoided considering the short-term repercussions of their actions. The fate of their reforms under the successor civilian governments is suggestive of the incompatibility, at least in the Turkish case, between democratic pluralism and rapid social reforms.

Nevertheless, the accomplishments of the NUC in social and economic fields should not be minimized. In particular, the revision of the tax system and the establishment of a planning board were of great potential significance. The effects of these reforms on the social and economic development of Turkey might have been substantial, had they not been reversed, halted, or watered down by the successor civilian administrations. It should also be noted that the intellectual climate for a coherent social reform program was lacking in Turkey in 1960. Indeed, the swing to the right with the transition to a pluralist system in 1946 and the suppression of all shades of political leftism, including "a good many ideas which in the West are generally accepted or at most can be labeled 'liberal,'" had prevented any serious discussion of even a moderate reform program.[64] Interestingly, problems of social reform came to the fore only after the Revolution of 1960, for which the NUC should be given credit. If its actions in relation to these problems were not as bold and imaginative as they could have been, it is hardly the military rulers of 1960–61 that should be blamed.

What is the basis for military leftism in Turkey? I earlier suggested that the answer could be found by examining (1) the economic hardships faced by the military under the Menderes regime and, even more importantly, (2) the social composition of the Turkish Army. Some scholars have expressed doubts about the value of social-background analysis in the study of the military. Janowitz, for example, has pointed out that "there are many steps between the impact of social origin and the political perspectives of a professional group. Especially in the military, the values of early socialization are refashioned by education and career experiences." Social and political behavior of the military in the middle of the twentieth century cannot therefore be explained by the pattern of social stratification alone. "Modern technology has produced such a high level of specialization," Janowitz contends, "that men are likely to think of themselves as members of a specific skill group, rather than as members of a social class. The growth of skill specialization produces professionalization, which, in turn, influences social and political perspectives."[65]

It has been generally admitted, however, that this assumption is more applicable to modern societies than to new nations. In developing countries social origin seems to play a much more significant role in shaping the political perspectives of the military.[66] Thus, it may be hypothesized that armies of lower- and lower-middle class origins are more likely to be a progressive force than armies of feudal or upper-class origins. The psychological mechanism through which social background influences political attitudes has been aptly described by Lucian Pye:

> Invariably the men, and sometimes even the officers, come from extremely humble circumstances, and it is only within the army that they are first introduced to the possibility of systematically advancing themselves. In transitional societies, where people's station in life is still largely determined by birth and by chance opportunities, powerful reactions usually follow from placing people in a position where they can recognize a definite and predictable relationship between effort and reward. The practice of giving advancement on merit can encourage people, first, to see the army as a just organization deserving of their loyalties, and then possibly to demand the same form of justice reign throughout their society.[67]

Data on the hypothesis stated above, however, do not seem to be conclusive. Lieuwen argues that in Latin America "today's officers are lower-middle class in social origin, but their institutional identification is so strong that it obliterates any meaningful identification with civilian social groups. Institutional considerations, the traditional insistence upon law and order, and the almost morbid fear of a social revolution that might destroy their organization combine in a political philosophy that is basically conservative."[68] Nevertheless, reformist coups experienced by many Latin American countries in the second quarter of the twentieth century were made by the military representatives of the new, middle-class urban groups which had no ties with either the landed oligarchy or the church hierarchy.[69]

A somewhat different account of the military in Latin America has been offered by John J. Johnson. In most parts of Latin America, he maintains, the historical alliances between the military and the landholding elite were dissolved, and "the officers have come to support the interests and aspirations of the urban propertied groups; the conservatism of the officers is of the same nature as that found in the urban middle sectors, and not, as is sometimes contended, the conservatism of the rural, landholding elite." He predicts, therefore, that as the officers are now "coming increasingly from the lower-middle sectors and the working

[27]

masses, the armed forces may be expected to be more inclined than formerly to gravitate toward positions identified with popular aspirations and to work with the representatives of the popular elements. . . ."[70] If this is the case, then the Latin American experience cannot be said to refute the argument linking the political attitudes of the military with its social origins.

In the Middle East, where military coups tended to be modernizing and reform-oriented, the army has become the principal actor and instrument of a new salaried, as opposed to property-owning, middle class.[71] Egyptian socialism, for example, cannot be explained without reference to the humble social origins of a great majority of Egyptian officers, as typified by Nasser, the son of a postmaster.[72] In Egypt, as General Nagib wrote, "except for the royal family, there was no aristocracy, and the sort of land-owners and traders who might have led the Armed Forces were too busy enjoying their wealth to be bothered with military service. The officer corps in consequence was largely composed of the sons of civil servants and the grandsons of peasants."[73]

The correspondence between political attitudes and social origin of the military is equally clear in the Turkish case. It is the consensus of Turkish and foreign observers that the Turkish officer corps is recruited, by and large, from the lower-middle and the salaried middle classes, for whom the military profession represents one of the few available channels of upward mobility.[74] What differentiates the elite from the masses in Turkey is, probably more than anything else, education. There is considerable opportunity for advancement beyond the *lycée* level.[75] Nevertheless, while education is free in public schools at all levels, it is still extremely difficult for a poor family to support the children for a long period of *lycée* and university education. Nor are there enough such schools, especially in outlying regions of Turkey. Technical and vocational education have long been neglected, and only recently has a conscious effort begun to divert the graduates of elementary and middle schools to vocational training. Under these circumstances, professional military schools, which provide free board, clothing, and other basic needs, are virtually the only place for a poor boy or even a middle-class son from a remote part of Turkey to obtain an education beyond the elementary school level. Furthermore, as was pointed out previously, the prestige of the military profession among high-income groups declined sharply during the Republic. These two factors combined to give the Turkish armed forces a distinctly lower-middle-class composition.

A study which I made of the social composition of the NUC tends to confirm this proposition. Of twenty-nine members of the NUC, for whom there is social-background data based on newspaper interviews, most came from lower-middle-class or salaried middle-class families: eight were sons of officers, six of civil servants, six of artisans and merchants, four of professionals, and two of farmers.[76] Furthermore, an attempt was made to determine the class position of their families depending on their life stories and other relevant social background information: at least eleven out of twenty-nine could safely be classified as belonging to lower or lower-middle-class families. Many members in this group referred to extreme hardships they suffered during childhood. The rest apparently came from what may be broadly defined as middle-class families. But even within the latter group, salaried personnel constituted the largest contingent. Close to half (seven out of fifteen) of the middle-class members whose fathers' professions are known were the sons of army officers or civil servants. None of the members appeared to belong to the top political or economic elite.[77] Finally, the NUC did not seem to over-represent metropolitan areas: only eleven out of the total membership of thirty-eight were born in one of the three large urban centers of Istanbul, Ankara, and Izmir.[78]

Clearly, social-background analysis in such a small group as the NUC is a hazardous task, and one may rightfully ask if the NUC is representative of the Turkish military in its social background. However, apart from the intrinsic value of studying the type of the military group which carried out a successful coup, the present analysis supports, within the limits of our sample, the generally held opinions about the social composition of the Turkish armed forces. As to the hypothesized relationship between the political attitudes and social origins of the military, needless to say that membership in a particular social class is by no means the only determinant of policy orientation. Yet, the Turkish experience again supports the hypothesis that armies recruited from lower social strata tend to be more socially progressive and reform-minded than armies of feudal or upper-class origins. Finally, the Turkish case suggests that military regimes need not always be unsuccessful in reforming their social and economic systems and providing economic direction to their nations.

[29]

III

The Dynamics of Military Intervention:
Military Radicals vs. Moderates

It has been argued that, although the occurrence of a successful military coup is essentially related to the functioning of the political system as a whole, the timing and the structure of the coup, and especially the attitudes of the new military government towards a return to constitutional normality, are largely determined by the internal dynamics of the military institution. Furthermore, this set of dynamics seems to follow a universal pattern. Thus, given the increasing size of military establishments and the increasing complexity of the governmental apparatus, a coup needs to involve a relatively large number of officers if it is to succeed; and, since the armed forces are likely to hold a variety of political orientations, this, in turn, requires the building of a coalition among various military factions of a size and character adequate to execute the successful coup. Apart from differences in political orientations, different thresholds to interventionism exist within this coalition. Naturally, the originators of the conspiracy have the lowest, and the last adherent or group of adherents to the movement the highest thresholds. Given the critical nature of the support provided by the latter, it is probable that one of the last adherents ("swing man") will be placed at the head of the military government that emerges from the successful coup. He is generally a high-ranking officer of great prestige (both within and outside the armed forces). "An interesting and paradoxical situation is thus created. The 'swing man' becomes the leading figure in the new government; yet he is the person who was least committed to the objectives of the coup, whose threshold to intervention was the highest of all the conspirators, and who was a last-minute addition to the conspiracy perhaps out of sympathy with, or not even aware of, the more

[30]

fundamental aims of the group that hatched the original plan."

The nature of the military coalition which carries out the coup tends to produce conflict within the new military government. While the "swing man" regards the objectives of the coup as realized with the overthrow of the former regime and favors an early return to civilian rule, the original instigators of the coup urge prolonged military rule and more fundamental social and political changes. In this conflict, the radicals normally have a good chance of prevailing over the moderates and preventing for an extended period the return to constitutionality. In fact, the logic of the situation seems to favor the radicals, for the restoration of constitutional procedures is likely to lead to the return to power of the supporters of the displaced government, and those who participated in the original coup must then reckon with the possibility of their vengeance. Consequently, the military "continues to play an active political role, if only for self-defence. 'Who rides the tiger can never dismount.' 'Whosoever draws his sword against the prince must throw the scabbard away.' These two proverbs pithily express the logic of the situation."[79] Huntington argued in the same vein that "each radical or conservative change in direction itself tends to be a complex event moving through several phases. In moderated and abbreviated form this pattern resembles the same phases through which major revolutionary upheavals usually proceed. . . . The critical seizure of power is . . . usually followed by one or more consolidating coups in which the original tendencies of the first coup are further strengthened."[80]

The dynamics of the Turkish coup of 1960 generally conformed to the pattern described above with the important difference that the military moderates prevailed over their radical comrades. This chapter will examine the planning and structure of the Turkish coup, with particular attention to the conflict within the Turkish armed forces over the question of civilian control. In addition, an attempt will be made to explain the somewhat unexpected outcome of this conflict.

Semi-conspiratorial military activities against the DP government began in 1954. These activities have been described in detail by other writers on the subject and need not be treated at length here.[81] It should be noted, however, that the first military clique was formed in November 1954 and that in the course of 1955 and 1956 this group became a well-organized secret society with Lieutenant Colonel Faruk Güventürk as President and Major Dündar Seyhan as Secretary-General. While the original aim of these dissident officers was to seek reform in the armed forces by securing the appointment of like-minded comrades, they soon concluded that only a military coup would solve the country's more basic problems. Thus, in 1957 some members of the group began to urge that a coup be attempted before the elections of that year. But the majority realized that the forces at their command were not yet sufficient to insure success. The arrest of Güventürk and eight other officers in the fall of 1957 on an unsubstantiated charge of conspiracy further delayed the action. In 1958 and 1959 the plotters concentrated on securing positions in the Army Personnel Office in order to manipulate assignments and on locating a high-ranking general to lead their organization. First, General Necati Tacan, the Commander of the Ground Forces, assented to the plans, and, after his death of a heart attack, his successor General Cemal Gürsel concurred. However, General Gürsel made it clear that a military coup should be staged only as a last resort.

While Gürsel's assistance and the control of the Personnel Office were invaluable assets for the plotters, they began to find themselves increasingly divided on the question of what to do if they should come to power. Some members, including Gürsel, insisted that a civilian Provisional Assembly be established and new elections be held within a few months. Others, led by Colonel Türkes, argued that a multi-party system would not bring about the rapid social and economic development Turkey so dearly needed, that radical social reforms would be necessary before the military could relinquish power.[82]

This issue, which remained unresolved in the planning stage of the coup, reasserted itself in the NUC period and continued to occupy the center of Turkish politics at least until after the last abortive coup of May 21, 1963. That the NUC was deeply divided over the question of returning power to civilians gradually became clear after May 27. The first serious conflict within the Committee arose over the appointment of cabinet ministers. While the moderates favored a cabinet composed of civilian experts, the radicals insisted that the ministries be assumed by the NUC members. Finally, a predominantly civilian cabinet, with only three ministerial posts occupied by military figures, was installed. The same issue again divided the NUC after the dismissal of ten of the original ministers in August 1960. The radicals repeated their proposal of a military cabinet which would be strong enough to carry out basic reforms, but the idea was rejected by the moderates by a margin of one vote.[83]

By the fall of 1960, several cliques had been formed within the NUC. Some eleven members were in favor of early elections; they also argued that the NUC should not become entangled in social reforms but should leave these matters to successor civilian governments. Some members of this group were believed to be in contact with the People's Party. Another group was composed of fifteen to twenty radicals who advocated the implementation of social reforms through a prolonged period of military rule. The remaining NUC members tried to exercise a balancing influence. Although they were not against a reform program to be carried out by the NUC, some felt it necessary to ally themselves with the first group, apparently out of their distrust of Colonel Türkeş.[84] In October 1960, a short-lived agreement was reached between the radicals and the moderates to the effect that every effort would be made to accomplish certain reforms by October 29, 1961, the date set for the elections. They also agreed that should this prove to be impossible, they would ask for a mandate from the people to stay in power for an additional four-year period.[85]

While this compromise was endorsed on October 25, 1960 by an overwhelming majority of the NUC, with only four members voting against it, mutual distrust between the moderates and the radicals continued. Finally, on November 13, General Gürsel announced the dismissal of fourteen members of the NUC, and reiterated the Committee's determination to set the nation back on a democratic road. Available evidence shows that this purge was carried out on the initiative of the senior members of the NUC and with the crucial support of the air force. It is clear, however, that a majority of the NUC members did not concur in this decision: only 16 out of 37 members had advance knowledge of the purge. The remaining seven members learned of the decision at the same time as their dismissed comrades. In fact, the seven had generally voted with the fourteen on many issues, and their inclusion in the dismissal list had been considered. This idea was rejected, however, on the ground that it would be inexpedient to admit that the majority of the Committee was on the side of the radicals.[86]

[33]

The purge cleared the road toward early elections, but it did not resolve the fundamental conflict within the armed forces on the future role of the military in the Turkish political system. After the elections of October 15, 1961, a group of high-ranking officers attempted to set aside the elections, to dissolve the newly elected Assembly before its opening, and to suspend all political parties. The Chief of the General Staff, General Cevdet Sunay, and the air force officers, on the other hand, argued that a coalition government headed by Inönü should be given a chance. The crisis was calmed by a number of concessions made by party leaders to the military. These included General Gürsel's election to the Presidency and the postponement of plans for an amnesty for the convicted DP leaders. Thus, the first civilian government of the Second Republic was formed by Inönü with the uneasy participation of the Justice Party.[87]

On February 22, 1962, the government very narrowly averted a new attempt at a coup. This attempt, led by Colonel Aydemir, involved not only "a group of young officers around the Military Academy" but also a substantial number of colonels and some generals.[88] Although the top military command and the air force were against the coup, the dissidents controlled almost all key units in Ankara and Istanbul. In their efforts to obtain the approval of the chief-of-staff, however, the insurgents made their plans known to the government. This gave the government and the top commanders enough time to appoint new officers to some of the key posts held by the insurgents and to order loyal units to move towards Ankara. After several hours of an apparent stalemate Aydemir agreed to call off action in exchange for an amnesty. In the following months sixty-nine officers who took part in the attempted coup were retired and many others were assigned to less active duties, although no other punitive measures were taken against them.[89]

On May 20–21, 1963, Talât Aydemir led another unsuccesssful attempt to overthrow the government. But this time the government was more determined to put an end to such actions. The insurrectionists were brought to trial before a military court, and two of their leaders (Aydemir and Gürcan) were sentenced to death. Yet these failures cannot be taken as conclusive proof of the growing confidence of the military in civilian leadership. It was disclosed during the trial that several other groups were also engaged in conspiratorial activities and although Aydemir and his supporters had conducted unity negotiations with these groups, no agreement could be reached on the question of leadership. Thus, a potentially significant merger failed to materialize.[90]

All these incidents clearly show that the Turkish armed forces decided to return to the barracks under considerable strain. They also demonstrate the existence of two strong opposing tendencies within the Turkish military as to the proper role of the army in politics. Since the Revolution of 1960 the idea of radical reforms under military auspices has constantly clashed with the concepts of military professionalism and civilian leadership. An attempt will be made in the concluding pages of this essay to interpret this conflict in perspective and to predict its outcome. The empirical question to be answered here is whether there are significant social background and attitudinal differences between military radicals and their moderate comrades.

The Turkish experience supports the hypothesis that the original instigators of a coup tend to be more radical than the late-comers. Thus, among the fourteen radicals purged in November 1960 were some of the founders of the first conspiratorial society and the masterminds of the 1960 coup: Orhan Kabibay, Orhan Erkanlı, and Alparslan Türkes. The abortive coup of February 22, 1962, was also led by a group of veteran conspirators whose organizational work can be traced back to as early as 1956: Talât Aydemir, Dündar Seyhan, Sükrü Ilkin, and Necati Ünsalan. On the other hand, some of the last adherents to the 1960 movement, especially General Cemal Madanoglu, played a crucial role in the exiling of the fourteen. Gürsel's position is somewhat different from that of a typical "swing man." As was noted above, he joined the group in 1959 and was not therefore a last-minute addition to the conspiracy. However, available evidence indicates that he was not in close contact with the other conspirators and had met only three of them before the coup. It is most likely that he was unaware of the long-term objectives of the radical group. Furthermore, because he was put on terminal leave at the beginning of May 1960, he did not play any role in the timing and execution of the coup.[91]

The most outstanding difference between the radicals and the moderates is probably that of age. The average age of the fourteen radical members of the NUC (as of 1960) was 36.8, and of the "Allied Group" (seven members who sympathized with the radicals), 38. By comparison, the average age of the moderates was 45.3. The radical group included no generals, one out of the eight colonels, three of the seven lieutenant colonels, five of the twelve majors, and five of the six captains. The allied group included one colonel, two lieutenant colonels, three majors, and one captain. Conversely, all five generals and six out of eight colonels were in the moderate group.[92] The generals also differed from their colleagues in their pattern of recruitment to the conspiracy: Gürsel was the only general connected with the group as of May 1960; three generals (Cemal Madanoglu, Irfan Bastug, and Sıtkı Ulay) joined the movement as late as the last two weeks of May; and the fifth member, Istanbul Martial Law Commander General Fahri Özdilek, joined the revolutionaries on May 27, only after he saw that the coup had been successful.[93] That the high-ranking officers tended to have higher thresholds to interventionism than their lower-ranking colleagues was clearly demonstrated in the incidents of February 22, 1962, and May 21, 1963. The first abortive coup was led by a group of colonels, and although some generals apparently sympathized with the movement the top military commanders remained loyal to the government. The second attempt involved the retired leaders of the February 22 movement and a group of even lower-ranking officers still on active service, with no participation by the top ranks of the military hierarchy.

What is the basis for this attitudinal difference between the senior and the junior officers? Edwin Lieuwen, after pointing out a similar division in Latin America's armies, argued that "generally opposed to the military 'reformers' were the senior officers. Their god was stability, and as its defenders they frowned upon social and political experimentation. . . . Their political philosophy was understandable. Having arrived at the top of their profession, they were affected by the conservatism that came with rank, age, status, and the attainment of comfortable material circumstances. The exalted rank of general enabled them, unlike the junior officers, to enter politics without sacrificing their professional position."[94] Another factor may be the gap between technical skills of senior officers and leadership skills of junior officers. "Senior officers, who must take charge of staff, command, and coordination, remain clients of the state—no matter how dysfunctioning." Thus, in certain developing countries, the army's increased efficiency and professionalization seem to have "intensified the social and chronological gap between senior and junior officers, and sharpened the latter's 'social consciousness.' While their superiors acted as bureaucratic managers, the junior officers assumed the role of leaders."[95]

Another interesting, but not readily explicable, attitudinal difference emerged between army and air force officers after the 1960 coup. The coup was executed with successful cooperation of land and air forces. An air force officer, Halim Mentes, had joined the conspiracy as early as 1957 and had formed a cell in the air force. Three other air force officers (Mucip Ataklı, Haydar Tunçkanat, and Emanullah Çelebi), who were to become members of the NUC, joined the group in early 1960. These officers and their colleagues at the Eskisehir air base played a crucial role in the arrest of Menderes on the morning of May 27. However, the three air force officers in the NUC were among the most ardent advocates of early elections. Of four members who voted against the October 25, 1960, compromise, three were these air force officers.[96] The air force also played a very important role in the purge of the fourteen and the suppression of the attempted coups in 1962 and 1963. Nevertheless, it should be noted that eleven high-ranking air force officers (including three generals and seven colonels) were retired on December 2, 1962, for insubordination and alleged contacts with former air force members of the NUC. This group is known to have been in touch with other conspiratorial groups before the plot of May 21, 1963. However, no agreement was reached with the Aydemir group, and although the leader of the air force group, ex-Colonel Halim Mentes, was brought to trial after the failure of the attempted coup, he received only a token sentence of ten months' imprisonment. No satisfactory explanation seems to exist for the attitudinal difference between army and air force officers. It is likely, therefore, that this difference is due, more than anything else, to skillfully exploited institutional rivalries.

What other characteristics differentiate military radicals from moderates? In view of the crudity of interview data, our conclusions can at best be highly tentative. But, as might be expected, radicals and moderates seem to differ in the extent to which they think in terms of social reforms. Almost all radical members of the NUC and their sympathizers, in contrast to less than half of the moderates, stressed social reforms among the most important problems of the country. The moderate group tended to emphasize education and secularism. However, some members of the latter group were quite as reform-minded as their radical colleagues. Similarly, distrust of political parties was more marked among the radicals and their allies than among the moderates. Six out of ten radicals (including the allied group), as opposed to only one out of five moderates, were of the opinion that necessary social reforms could not be carried out by parties.

How are we to explain the failure of the radical officers in Turkey? In what ways, if any, was the Turkish experience different from the experience of other countries where the radicals prevailed over their moderate colleagues? Perhaps a crucial difference is that in Turkey, contrary to the case of many other developing countries, not all civilian political leaders and institutions were discredited at the time of the Revolution. In particular, the PRP was able to avoid such a fate, and its leader, Ismet Inönü, himself a veteran military hero, was widely popular in the armed forces. The presence of Gürsel and Inönü at the head of government during the first three years of post-revolutionary civilian rule provided a strong guarantee against a new military intervention. Secondly, it was generally believed after the 1960 coup that the DP had lost much of its popular strength. The results of the constitutional referendum of July 9, 1960, helped to strengthen this belief. While the supporters of the DP voted against the Constitution, the percentage of the "no" votes (38.3 per cent) fell far short of a popular majority. Therefore, the PRP came to the election of October 1961 with full confidence that it would win a majority.[97] Furthermore, there were reasons to hope that the losing party would gain respectability by drastic modification of its program and tactics. Thus, almost all the leaders of the DP were driven out of politics by death or imprisonment. The successor parties were led by more acceptable personalities, in the view of the military, than the former Democratic leaders: the JP by retired general Ragıp Gümüşpala, the first Chief of Staff under the NUC government; and the NTP by Ekrem Alican, the first Minister of Finance in the NUC cabinet. While some elements in the military were dissatisfied with the results of the 1961 elections, the situation was still far from alarming. The JP had won only 34.8 per cent of the popular vote and 35.1 per cent of the Assembly seats. It should also be noted that the repeated pledges by the JP leaders to work in the "spirit of May 27" convinced some military leaders that the shift towards respectability was genuine. By the time it was clear that the JP was a continuation of the DP and strong enough to win an absolute majority in the Assembly, it was too late to effect a basic reversal of direction. The radicals, having tried and failed twice, had lost their once strong position in the armed forces. The military commanders, by crushing the uprisings in 1962 and 1963, had also committed themselves to support the existing regime. Thus, a new precarious balance emerged between the military and the political tendency it temporarily ousted from power in 1960. The nature of this equilibrium may well be the key to future political developments in Turkey.

IV

Conclusion

One of the proclaimed aims of the Turkish Revolution of 1960 was to remove from Turkish political life the total antagonism between the Democrats and Republicans, to extricate these parties, in the words of the first pronunciamento of the NUC, "from the irreconcilable situation into which they have fallen." The Revolution failed, however, to alleviate this polarization which had led to a paralysis of the political system in 1960. If anything, the reverse seems to have occurred. The bitter partisan enmity of the 1950s, which was nevertheless largely devoid of ideological content, has been further intensified by increasing ideological polarization. On the one hand, the conservative but essentially pragmatic outlook of the Democrats has given way to the more ideology-conscious business conservatism of the JP. The Republicans, on the other hand, have tended to stress statism, economic planning, and social justice. Despite the resistance of the conservative elements in the party, the PRP leadership seems to be determined to pursue a left-of-center policy. Further to the left, the rising interest in socialism has been marked by the appearance of the Turkish Workers' Party, a highly vocal Marxist group which won 3 per cent of the popular vote in the 1965 elections. Finally, the Republican Peasants Nation Party changed, under the leadership of Alparslan Türkes into a national socialist party, while the Nation Party and New Turkey Party have tended to take a center-right position.

The antagonism between private enterprise and social justice has become the axis of Turkish politics. This cleavage is exacerbated by the superimposition of a division of opinion on foreign policy. Although the value of friendship with the West is not seriously questioned, Turkish parties differ in their opinion as to the nature of this friendship. The PRP, the TWP, the RPNP, and the NP advocate, in varying forms and degrees, a more independent foreign policy, and criticize the JP for being excessively pro-American. The JP government has often been accused of losing sight of Turkish national interests and following a policy of political, economic, and military dependence on the United States. In short, there seems to be a growing consensus among the groups which formerly opposed the Menderes regime on a socially progressive, but not necessarily socialist, economic policy and a more independent and flexible, but not necessarily neutralist, foreign policy.

In view of the distinctly reformist outlook of the Turkish military which has been described above, we may assume that a majority of Turkish officers are in sympathy with the reform elements in the political system. It is also likely that the call for an independent foreign policy will appeal to the highly nationalistic officer corps. This, in turn, poses a major dilemma for Turkish democracy, for the circumstances of Turkish political development have brought conservative, not reform, tendencies to a clear predominance. As Weiker rightly observed: "When given the free ballot, the Turkish nation has not at any time in the past voted for the representatives of rapid reform, and there are convincing reasons for believing that such an eventuality is equally unlikely today."[98] Theoretically, this dilemma can be resolved in several ways. The JP can, for example, adjust itself to the aspirations of the reformist groups. Given its "insulating power base" in the rural areas, however, this party has little or no electoral incentive to seek a compromise with its adversaries, nor has it so far shown any willingness to do so. Another long-term possibility is the gradual disintegration of the conservative popular majority, or a shift in the distribution of popular opinion to the advantage of the reformist groups. Particularly, the growing urban working classes may shift their loyalties from the explicitly pro-business JP to one of the pro-labor parties. Nevertheless, it is not certain whether the loss of urban labor support will deprive the JP of its popular majority, as long as Turkey remains an essentially agrarian country and the JP retains its rural strongholds. A change in the voting patterns of the rural population is least likely because of the traditional conservatism of the Turkish villagers and the political, economic, and intellectual influence of the ultra-conservative land-owning and commercial elites on the bulk of the peasantry. If, however, none of these democratic solutions to the present

[41]

impasse works out; if, in Weiker's words, "the revamped political structure of Turkey's Second Republic proves unworkable as the basis for economic and social progress," another period of military tutelage may have considerable appeal to the military and the civilian reformists as the only alternative to an indefinite period of conservative rule.[99]

The Turkish coup of 1960 and the NUC rule that followed should be interpreted as a certain stage of the century-old virulent conflict between the radicals and the conservatives. The coup represented a temporary but still significant victory for the radicals. Although it did not attempt to make fundamental social and economic reforms, it nevertheless produced certain necessary policy changes in these fields. It would be wrong, therefore, to view the 1960 coup as "backward looking" or as "the intelligentsia's reaction against democracy and particularly its egalitarian effects." The coup did not aim at "forestalling . . . the crumbling of the traditional social order, based on the supremacy of the urban classes and particularly of the intelligentsia."[100] The groups which made and supported the 1960 Revolution did not want to restore a status quo based on their old privileges. They sought to effect a more balanced economic growth and a more equitable distribution of wealth, upon which alone a healthy democracy could be built. They did not attempt to limit the participation of the peasantry in politics; they tried to make such participation more effective and meaningful. The ultimate success of the Second Turkish Republic may well depend on its capacity to solve the same problems.

Notes

1. These are the Turkish Workers' Party (TWP) and the Republican Peasants Nation Party (RPNP). While the latter retained the name of the old RPNP, it is now firmly controlled by some former members of the NUC, under the leadership of ex-Colonel Alparslan Türkes. The bulk of the membership of the old RPNP followed their veteran leader, Osman Bölükbası, to the Nation Party (NP). The Justice Party (JP) and the New Turkey Party (NTP) were also created after the revolution. The former is essentially a continuation of the Democratic Party (DP) while the NTP can be considered the successor of the Freedom Party. For details, see pp. 40-41.

2. See pp. 40-42.

3. Frederick W. Frey, *The Turkish Political Elite* (Cambridge, Mass.: M.I.T. Press, 1965), p. 6.

4. Martin C. Needler, "Political Development in Latin America: Instability, Violence, and Evolutionary Change," forthcoming, Chap. 4.

5. Samuel P. Huntington, "Political Development and Political Decay," *World Politics*, Vol. XVII (April, 1965), pp. 386–430.

6. *Ibid.*, p. 427; Fred R. Von Der Mehden, *Politics of the Developing Nations* (Englewood Cliffs, N.J.: Prentice-Hall, 1964), p. 65.

7. S. E. Finer, *The Man on Horseback: The Role of the Military in Politics* (London and Dunmow: Pall Mall Press, 1962), Chaps. 7–9, esp. p. 139.

8. Samuel P. Huntington, *The Soldier and the State: The Theory and Politics of Civil-Military Relations* (New York: Random House Vintage Books Edition, 1964), pp. 70–78, 83–85.

9. Frey, *op. cit.*, pp. 301–3. A national survey of the peasant population of Turkey in 1962 carried out by Frey and his associates indicated that "prior to the abolition of village-level party cells (*ocaklar*) under the military junta of 1960–61, about two-thirds of the villagers of Turkey lived in communities which had local party organizations. Furthermore, over three-fifths lived in villages where *more than one* party had such a local organization." (*Ibid.*, p. 375, n. 12.)

[43]

10. Huntington, "Political Development and Political Decay," pp. 394–99.

11. Dankwart A. Rustow, "Turkey's Second Try at Democracy," *Yale Review*, Vol. LII (Summer, 1963), pp. 528–29.

12. On the political implications of rapid social mobilization, see Huntington, "Political Development and Political Decay," pp. 402–3, 415–21; Karl Deutsch, "Social Mobilization and Political Development," *American Political Science Review*, Vol. LV (September, 1961), pp. 493–514.

13. Frey, *op. cit.*, p. 391.

14. See, in general, William Kornhauser, *The Politics of Mass Society* (Glencoe: Free Press, 1963).

15. On the depoliticization of the army under Atatürk, see Frederick W. Frey, "Arms and the Man in Turkish Politics," *Land Reborn*, Vol. XI (August, 1960), pp. 5–6; George S. Harris, "The Role of the Military in Turkish Politics," (Part I), *Middle East Journal*, Vol. XIX (Winter, 1965), pp. 54–61; Dankwart A. Rustow, "The Army and the Founding of the Turkish Republic," *World Politics*, Vol. XI (July, 1959), pp. 543–52; Daniel Lerner and Richard D. Robinson, "Swords and Ploughshares: The Turkish Army as a Modernizing Force," *World Politics*, Vol. XV (October, 1960), pp. 19–22. On the historical and religious roots of military rule in the Middle East, see Sydney Nettleton Fisher, "The Role of the Military in Society and Government in Turkey," in Fisher (ed.), *The Military in the Middle East* (Columbus: Ohio State University Press, 1963), pp. 22–23; Dankwart A. Rustow, "The Military in Middle Eastern Society and Politics," *ibid.*, pp. 8–9; Manfred Halpern, "Middle Eastern Armies and the New Middle Class," in John J. Johnson (ed.), *The Role of the Military in Underdeveloped Countries* (Princeton: Princeton University Press, 1962), pp. 277–78; Edward Shils, "The Military in the Political Development of the New States," in Johnson (ed.), *op. cit.*, pp. 52–53.

16. Frey, "Arms and the Man in Turkish Politics," pp. 7–8.

17. Bernard Lewis also says that the Kemalist "regime, though military in its origin and for a long time authoritarian in character, was never a mere military dictatorship" (*The Emergence of Modern Turkey* [London: Oxford University Press, 1961], p. 364). For the concept of "praetorian regimes" see David C. Rapoport, "A Comparative Theory of Military and Political Types," in Samuel P. Huntington (ed.), *Changing Patterns of Military Politics* (New York: Free Press, 1962), pp. 72–74.

[44]

18. Ali Fuad Basgil, *La Révolution Militaire de 1960 en Turquie* (Geneva: Editions Perret-Gentil, 1963), pp. 185–201.

19. Lerner and Robinson, *op. cit.*, p. 42; Von Der Mehden, *op. cit.*, p. 101.

20. For the role of Gürsel in the making of the coup, see pp. 00–00.

21. Lucian W. Pye, "Armies in the Process of Political Modernization," in Johnson (ed.), *The Role of the Military in Underdeveloped Countries*, pp. 73–80.

22. Lerner and Robinson, *op. cit.*, pp. 27–41.

23. Harris, *op. cit.*, p. 61.

24. For a similar observation on the Kemalist era, see Fisher, *op. cit.*, p. 29. A 1959 survey of the value systems of *lycée*-level students (i.e., those of regular *lycées*, commercial *lycées*, teacher-training schools, boys' vocational schools, and girls' vocational schools) in Turkey strongly supports this argument. The distribution of responses by regular *lycée* students to the question: "For which vocation do you, personally, feel the greatest respect?" is as follows: free professions: 55.9 per cent; education: 14.4 per cent; government and politics: 13.1 per cent; military: 11.3 per cent; business and commerce: 2.4 per cent; others: 2.9 per cent. The same distribution for the total sample is as follows: free professions: 44.4 per cent; education: 23.2 per cent; government and politics: 10.6 per cent; business and commerce: 9.5 per cent; military: 9.11 per cent; others: 3.2 per cent. Furthermore, it has been observed that the prestige attributed to the military profession tends to vary *inversely* with the economic well-being of the respondents' families. See Frederick W. Frey, George W. Angell, and Abdurrahman S. Sanay, *Ögrencilerin Meslek Gruplarına Bagladiklari Degerler* ("Values Attributed by Students to Vocational Categories") (Ankara: Millî Egitim Bakanlıgı Talim ve Terbiye Dairesi Egitim Arastirmaları ve Degerlendirme Merkezi, 1962), *passim*, but esp. pp. 12–14, 38–44.

25. Frey, *The Turkish Political Elite*, pp. 390, 260–61; also his "Arms and the Man in Turkish Politics," *op. cit.*

26. Frey, *The Turkish Political Elite*, pp. 180–83, 280–82, and *passim*.

27. Morris Janowitz, *The Military in the Political Development of New States: An Essay in Comparative Analysis* (Chicago: University of Chicago Press, 1964), pp. 65–66; also Halpern, *op. cit.*, pp. 300–3.

28. Frey, *The Turkish Political Elite*, pp. 395–96; Harold D. Lasswell, Daniel Lerner, and C. Easton Rothwell, *The Comparative Study*

of Elites (Stanford: Stanford University Press, 1952), p. 16; J. F. S. Ross, *Parliamentary Representation* (New Haven: Yale University Press, 1944), p. 115. For the political power of the military and various patterns of civil-military relations, see Huntington, *The Soldier and the State*, pp. 86–89, 96–97. For a comparison of civil-military relations in the United States and the Soviet Union, see Zbigniew Brzezinski and Samuel P. Huntington, *Political Power: USA/USSR* (New York: Viking Press Compass Books Edition, 1965), Chap. 8. For the representation of the military in the French government, see Mattei Dogan, "Political Ascent in a Class Society: French Deputies 1870–1958," in Dwaine Marvick (ed.), *Political Decision-makers* (Glencoe: Free Press, 1961), pp. 67, 73.

29. Frey notes that "the importance of the military men's feeling that they had lost 'their representatives' among the deputies" is "graphically recorded in the reports of the planning of the coup" (*The Turkish Political Elite*, p. 390). There is very little evidence for this feeling, however, in the sources he cited. See Abdi Ipekçi and Ömer Sami Cosar, *Ihtilâlin Içyüzü* ("The Inside Story of the Revolution") (Istanbul: Uygun Yayınevi, 1965), esp. pp. 11–195. Similarly, in the interviews with the NUC members by the Turkish newspaper *Cumhuriyet* published between July 16 and August 23, 1960, decline of military political power was hardly mentioned as a major source of disenchantment with the DP regime. An English translation of these interviews is also available: Cevat F. Baskut, Yasar Kemal, and Ecvet Güresin, *Interviews with Members of Turkey's National Unity Committee* (U.S. Joint Publications Research Service, 1960). Quotations from these interviews are based on this translation unless otherwise indicated.

30. Dankwart A. Rustow, "The Military: Turkey," in Robert E. Ward and D. A. Rustow (eds.), *Political Modernization in Japan and Turkey* (Princeton: Princeton University Press, 1964), pp. 369–70, 372; also his "Turkey's Second Try at Democracy," p. 523; Finer, *op. cit.*, pp. 27, 117; Lerner and Robinson, *op. cit.*, p. 41; Walter F. Weiker, *The Turkish Revolution 1960–1961: Aspects of Military Politics* (Washington, D.C.: Brookings Institution, 1963), pp. 13–20; Nuri Eren *Turkey Today — And Tomorrow* (New York: Praeger, 1963), pp. 27, 34–39; Selâhattin Tansel, *27 Mayıs Inkilâbını Hazırlayan Sebepler* ("The Causes of the Revolution of May 27") (Istanbul: Millî Egitim Basımevi, 1960).

31. For a discussion of the unconstitutionality of the law conferring extraordinary authority on the Investigating Committee, see Ergun Özbudun, *Parlâmanter Rejimde Parlâmentonun Hükûmeti Murakabe Vasitaları* ("The Means of Parliamentary Control of the

Executive in the Parliamentary Government System) (Ankara: Ankara Universitesi Basımevi, 1962), pp. 114–16. Robinson, however, argues that, given the vagueness of the Turkish Constitution, the unconstitutionality of such restrictive laws was not clear: Richard D. Robinson, *The First Turkish Republic: A Case Study in National Development* (Cambridge, Mass.: Harvard University Press, 1963), pp. 256–57.

32. For the text of this letter, see *Cumhuriyet*, June 14, 1960; a summary of it is given by Weiker, *op. cit.*, pp. 121–22.

33. The following quotations from the *Cumhuriyet* interviews referred to in note 29, are germane: "The Kayseri incidents and then the university incidents, and the tragic pressure on the press and the jailings had moulded opinions. Matters reached a point where, in spite of my belief that the army should not participate in this matter, I did not see how the country could be saved without the army's intervention" (General Gürsel); "My heart, like that of every citizen, suffered . . . when the laws and even the Constitution were trampled on, and when the nation and its youth began to be beaten. We even began to be ashamed of the weapons in our hands" (General Ulay). See also the interviews with Colonel Köksal, Colonel Küçük, Colonel Tunçkanat, Major Celebi, and Major Özkaya.

34. For the text of this declaration, see Robinson, *op. cit.*, pp. 255–56.

35. Janowitz, *op. cit.*, p. 37.

36. Huntington, *The Soldier and the State*, pp. 77–78.

37. Frey, *The Turkish Political Elite*, pp. 162, 261.

38. Ipekçi and Cosar, *op. cit.*, pp. 14–24; Harris, *op. cit.*, pp. 63–65.

39. *Ibid.*, p. 66; Ipekçi and Cosar, *op. cit.*, pp. 14–15, 23–24.

40. Baskut, Kemal, and Güresin, *op. cit.* The same theme (i.e., the betrayal of the Atatürk Revolution) is stressed in almost all interviews. See also Ipekçi and Cosar, *op. cit.*, pp. 25–26, 33, 50.

41. Frey, *The Turkish Political Elite*, p. 180.

42. On the questions of secularism and religious revival in Turkey, see Niyazi Berkes, *The Development of Secularism in Turkey* (Montreal: McGill University Press, 1964); Lewis V. Thomas, "Recent Developments in Turkish Islam," *Middle East Journal*, Vol. VI (Winter, 1952), pp. 22–40; Howard A. Reed, "Revival of Islam in Secular Turkey," *ibid.*, Vol. VIII (Summer, 1954), pp. 267–82; "The Religious Life of Modern Turkish Muslims," in Richard N. Frye (ed.), *Islam and the West* (Gravenhage: Mouton, 1957), pp. 108–48; "Secularism and

Islam in Turkish Politics," *Current History,* Vol. XXXII (June, 1957), pp. 333–38; Dankwart A. Rustow, "Politics and Islam in Turkey, 1920–1955," in Frye (ed.), *Islam and the West,* pp. 69–107; Bernard Lewis, "Islamic Revival in Turkey," *International Affairs,* Vol. XXVIII (January, 1952), pp. 38–48; Uriel Heyd, "Islam in Modern Turkey," *Journal of the Royal Central Asian Society,* Vol. XXXIV (July-Oct., 1947), pp. 299–308; Kemal H. Karpat, *Turkey's Politics: The Transition to a Multi-Party System* (Princeton: Princeton University Press, 1959), Chap. 10. For an essentially legal analysis of Turkish secularism, see Bülent Daver, *Türkiye Cumhuriyetinde Lâiklik* ("Secularism in Republican Turkey") (Ankara, 1955). For a summary and analysis of reactionary activities in the 1950s, see Tarık Z. Tunaya, *Islâmcılık Cereyanı* ("The Current of Islamism") (Istanbul: Baha Matbaasi, 1962).

43. Robinson, for example, argues that "by 1960, despite a religiously conservative element of politically significant size, it no longer endangered the secular republican state. Islam itself had been undergoing a subtle transformation even on the village level. Economic incentive, material well-being, innovation, the machine, commerce, and social change no longer appeared as challenges to religion. . . . An accommodation between folk Islam and modern life was in fact taking place" (*op. cit.,* p. 205). Similarly, the initial findings of a national survey of peasant attitudes carried out by Frey and others suggested that "there does not seem to be a hard attitudinal shell of ideological resistance to change among Turkish villagers. When the pressure for innovation is sufficiently strong so as to provoke open conflict, the chances for at least superficial victory for the modernizers should be quite good." However, in one of the published parts of this report, mass media exposure (certainly an important index of modernization) has been found to be negatively related with religious saliency. Frederick W. Frey, *The Mass Media and Rural Development in Turkey* (Rural Development Research Project Report No. 3 [M.I.T. Center For International Studies, 1966]), pp. 120, 129, 187.

44. Karpat, *op. cit.,* p. 288.

45. *Ibid.,* pp. 271, 277. For this view, see Ali Fuad Basgil, *Din ve Lâiklik* ("Religion and Secularism") (Istanbul, 1955). For a Kemalist interpretation of secularism, see Cetin Özek, *Türkiye'de Lâiklik* ("Secularism in Turkey") (Istanbul, 1962); also his "Türk Anayasa Hukukunda Lâiklik Kurali ve Gelisimi" ("The Principle of Secularism and Its Development in Turkish Constitutional Law"), *Istanbul Hukuk Fakültesi Mecmuasi,* Vol. XXVII (1961), pp. 96–207.

46. For the attitude of the NUC toward Islam and secularism, see Friedrich-Wilhelm Fernau, "Le Néo-Kémalisme du Comité d'Unité

Nationale," *Orient*, No. 16 (1960), pp. 56–58. Thus, General Gürsel described Islam as the crown of religions (Erzurum speech of October 25, 1960). Many members of the NUC advocated the training of enlightened clergymen and the Turkification of the Koran. See the interviews with Colonel Türkes, Colonel Köksal, Colonel Küçük, Captain Karavelioglu, Colonel Yurdakuler. Captain Özdag was most outspoken on this matter: "As long as Turkish reformers do not enter the mosque [community] as believers, they cannot make the peasant accept their ideas. Teachers, officials and others will have to descend to the people, become part of the mosque community, and attempt from that position to enlighten the people" (*Cumhuriyet*, July 24, 1960).

47. Frey, *The Turkish Political Elite*, p. 183 and *passim*.

48. Frank Tachau, "Provincial Party Organizations in Turkey," paper presented to the "Conference on Social Growth and Democracy in Turkey," held at New York University, May 27–29, 1965, Table III and *passim*. Interestingly, while all of the members of the JP provincial executive committee in Adana are professionals, half of their fathers' professions were in commerce or industry and half were in farming (*ibid.*, p. 10), thereby implying their presumably continuing interest in business and land ownership. This pattern, if it can be generalized, explains the socially ultra-conservative policies of a party whose national elite is seemingly dominated by professional people.

49. Nermin Abadan, *Anayasa Hukuku ve Siyasî Bilimler Açısından 1965 Seçimlerinin Tahlili* ("The Analysis of the 1965 Elections from the Angle of Constitutional Law and Political Science") (Ankara: Sevinç Matbaası, 1966), pp. 318–20.

50. Frey, *The Turkish Political Elite*, pp. 374–75. Thus, the Freedom Party movement signified a break of the intellectual and professional elements with the Democrats. Rustow, however, argued that the businessmen suffered from "clumsy and multifarious regulations under the Menderes regime," and they were "demanding greater freedom for private initiative" ("Turkey's Second Try at Democracy," pp. 529–30). Lerner and Robinson also cite the "entrepreneurs" among the groups alienated by the Democrats (*op. cit.*, p. 41).

51. Karpat, *op. cit.*, pp. 117–25, esp. 121–23.

52. For an account of this back-bench revolt, see Sarah P. Mc-Cally, "Party Government in Turkey," *Journal of Politics*, Vol. XVIII (May, 1956), pp. 297–323.

53. Karpat, *op. cit.*, p. 306. However, in his two recent articles, Karpat seems to give greater credit to the Democrats. See his "Recent

Political Developments in Turkey and Their Social Background," *International Affairs,* Vol. XXXVIII (July, 1962), pp. 304–23; and "Society, Economics, and Politics in Contemporary Turkey," *World Politics,* Vol. XVII (October, 1964), pp. 50–74.

54. William H. Nicholls, "Investment in Agriculture in Underdeveloped Countries," *American Economic Review,* Vol. XLV (May, 1955), pp. 64, 71.

55. Baskut, Kemal, and Güresin, *op. cit.* These nineteen members are Baykal, Celebi, Erkanlı, Ersü, Esin, Gürsoytrak, M. Kaplan, Karaman, Karan, Karavelioglu, Küçük, Özdag, Özdilek, Özgünes, Özgür, Özkaya, Solmazer, Soyuyüce, and Yildiz. It should be noted that these newspaper interviews were not certainly carried out with scientific rigour. While all the members were asked basically the same questions, emphasis on specific questions and answers varied depending on the personality of the interviewers and interviewees. Therefore, the failure of some members to mention social reforms and social justice among the most important problems of the country cannot be taken as decisive proof of their opposition or indifference to such reforms. On the discontent of the Turkish military with the economic policies of the Democrats, see also Ipekçi and Cosar, *op. cit.,* pp. 26, 50, 167, 250.

56. Huntington, *The Soldier and the State,* Chaps. 3–4, esp. pp. 93–94; see also Morris Janowitz, *The Professional Soldier: A Social and Political Portrait* (New York: Free Press, 1964), pp. 22–24.

57. Lucian W. Pye, *Aspects of Political Development* (Boston: Little, Brown, 1966), p. 173. Martin Needler observes that in Latin America, the trend is toward conservative coups: while in the decade 1935–1944 half of the coups were reformist, only 17 per cent in the decade 1955–64 could be so termed (*op. cit.*). On the Latin American experience, see also Edwin Lieuwen, "The Military: A Force for Continuity or Change," in John TePaske and Sydney N. Fisher (eds.), *Explosive Forces in Latin America* (Columbus: Ohio State University Press, 1964), p. 77; Lieuwen, *Generals vs. Presidents: Neomilitarism in Latin America* (New York: Praeger, 1964), pp. 100–106. In the Middle East, on the other hand, the military is essentially a force for progress.

58. Janowitz, *The Military in the Political Development of New States,* pp. 78–80; Rustow, "The Military in Middle Eastern Society and Politics," pp. 18–19; Amos Perlmutter, "The Politics of Emerging Arab Army Elites: A Comparative Demonstration," unpublished paper presented to the Harvard-MIT Joint Faculty Seminar on Political Development, March 23, 1966, p. 6.

59. Shils, *op. cit.,* pp. 55–56.

60. Samuel P. Huntington, "Patterns of Violence in World Politics," in Huntington (ed.), *Changing Patterns of Military Politics*, pp. 32–34. For a similar classification, see Von Der Mehden, *op. cit.*, pp. 99–106.

61. Article 129 of the 1961 Turkish Constitution states that: "Economic, social and cultural development is based on a plan. Development is carried out according to this plan.

"The organization and functions of the State Planning Organization, the principles to be observed in the preparation and execution, and application and revision of the plan, and the measures designed to prevent changes tending to impair the unity of the plan, shall be regulated by special legislation."

62. For an account of the economic reforms of the NUC, see Weiker, *op. cit.*, pp. 143–52; Fernau, *op. cit.*, pp. 61–65.

63. Weiker, *op. cit.*, pp. 148, 152–53, 157–58.

64. Karpat, *Turkey's Politics*, pp. 149–51 and Chap. 14.

65. Janowitz, *The Military in the Political Development of New States*, p. 56; also his *The Professional Soldier*, p. 7.

66. Shils, *op. cit.*, pp. 17–18, 24–25; Janowitz, *The Military in the Political Development of New States*, pp. 56–58.

67. Pye, *Aspects of Political Development*, pp. 182–83.

68. Lieuwen, *Generals vs. Presidents*, p. 104.

69. Edwin Lieuwen, *Arms and Politics in Latin America* (New York: Praeger, 1960), Chaps. 3 and 5, and esp. p. 126.

70. John J. Johnson, *The Military and Society in Latin America* (Stanford: Stanford University Press, 1964), pp. 149-52.

71. Manfred Halpern, *The Politics of Social Change in the Middle East and North Africa* (Princeton: Princeton University Press Paperback Edition, 1965), Chaps. 4 and 13.

72. Morroe Berger, *Military Elite and Social Change: Egypt since Napoleon* (Research Monograph No. 6 [Princeton University Center of International Studies, 1960]), pp. 2, 20; also P. J. Vatikiotis, *The Egyptian Army in Politics: Pattern For New Nations?* (Bloomington: Indiana University Press, 1961), pp. 46, 214–15.

73. Mohammed Nagib, *Egypt's Destiny* (New York, 1955), pp. 14–15.

74. Fisher, *op. cit.*, p. 29; Lewis, *The Emergence of Modern Turkey*, p. 457; Frey, *The Turkish Political Elite*, p. 138, n. 5.

75. Rustow, "The Military: Turkey," p. 386. On the importance of education in Turkish social and political systems, see also Frey, *The Turkish Political Elite*, Chap. 3; and his "Education: Turkey," in Ward and Rustow (eds.), *Political Modernization in Japan and Turkey*, pp. 205–35.

76. The remaining three were classified as unknown. My classification is somewhat different from Weiker's. He asserts that "of 27 for whom we have data, 12 are the sons of army officers, 4 of civilian government employees, 4 of businessmen, and 7 miscellaneous" (*op. cit.*, p. 118). In cases where two occupations were given, I chose the seemingly more permanent and essential one. If a man was both a farmer and a merchant or artisan, for example, I classified him as a merchant or artisan. The reason was that such a man would probably have rather different perspectives from one who was strictly a farmer.

77. Actually, the contingent of officers from lower-middle-class families may be much larger. The distinction between the terms "lower middle class" and "middle class" is not firmly established in Turkish, and the Turkish word, *ortahalli*, which was frequently used in these interviews, may mean either of them. To prevent a bias towards my argument I included all doubtful cases in the "middle class" category. It should also be pointed out that all members of the "merchant" contingent were small town or village traders, and some of them obviously belonged to the lower-middle class. Finally, the description of some civil servants and officers as members of the lower-middle class in a country where these groups have dominated the political system for centuries should not be seen as paradoxical. There are certainly great differences, in terms of power, status, and income, between upper and lower levels of the military and civilian hierarchies. Furthermore, the economic power of the officers and civilian bureaucrats declined sharply in the last two decades as a result of the inflation.

78. Weiker, *op. cit.*, p. 118.

79. Finer, *op. cit.*, pp. 118–19. The last two paragraphs rely heavily upon Martin Needler's perceptive forthcoming book cited in note 4.

80. Huntington, "Patterns of Violence in World Politics," p. 37.

81. Ipekçi and Cosar, *op. cit.*, pp. 24–229; a convenient summary of these events has been given by George S. Harris in "The Role of the Military in Turkish Politics" (Part II), *Middle East Journal*, Vol. XIX (Spring, 1965), pp. 169–76.

82. Ipekçi and Cosar, *op. cit.*, pp. 112–13, 124–29, 167.

83. *Ibid.*, pp. 258–59, 339, 383–86.

84. *Ibid.*, pp. 250–52, 381–86, 426–28.

85. *Ibid.*, pp. 438–41.

86. *Ibid.*, pp. 490–508. These seven members were Muzaffer Yurdakuler, Suphi Karaman, Ahmet Yildiz, Kadri Kaplan, Mehmet Özgünes, Selâhattin Özgür, and Kâmil Karavelioglu. In the analysis which follows, this group will be called the "Allied Group" to indicate their sympathy with the fourteen radicals. Weiker observed that "not many weeks passed before NUC members were taking pains to state that the fourteen were not really traitors, that the remaining members of the NUC considered them brothers in ideals. It is not unlikely that most of the NUC members soon developed doubts about the wisdom of what they had done" (*op. cit.*, p. 135). It is more likely, however, that such contradictory statements were due to the division within the purged NUC rather than to a change of attitude toward the exiles.

87. Can Kaya Isen, *22 Subat–21 Mayis: Geliyorum Diyen Ihtilâl* ("February 22–May 21: The Revolution That Said It Was Coming") (Istanbul: Tan Gazetesi ve Matbaasi, 1964), pp. 18–22. The protocol of October 21, 1960, urging the necessity for military intervention, was signed at the War Academy in Istanbul by ten generals and twenty-eight colonels. This protocol was also approved and signed by a group of generals and colonels who met at the Mürted air base near Ankara. However, after the intercession of General Sunay some generals wavered and the October 21 decision was abandoned. Weiker notes that the reversal of this decision "was made partly on the premise that action ought to be suspended since 'internal and external response to such intervention would be more favorable if it had been established that coalition government had not been successful.'" See Walter F. Weiker, "The Aydemir Case and Turkey's Political Dilemma," *Middle Eastern Affairs*, Vol. XIV (November, 1963), p. 263.

88. Weiker, *The Turkish Revolution, 1960–1961*, pp. 137–38; also Fisher, *op. cit.*, p. 38.

89. Isen, *op. cit.*, pp. 27–74.

90. *Ibid.*, pp. 75–131; Weiker, "The Aydemir Case and Turkey's Political Dilemma," pp. 265–66.

91. On Gürsel's role in the making of the 1960 coup, see Ipekçi and Cosar, *op. cit.*, *passim.* In fact, after Gürsel was put on leave and went to Izmir, he was kept under government surveillance. For this reason, the plotters decided to avoid contact with him.

92. General Irfan Bastug was killed in an automobile accident in September. There is evidence that he was one of the moderates. See Ipekçi and Cosar, *op. cit.*, p. 381.

93. Generals Özdilek and Sunay were contacted by the revolutionaries in May. They both refused to join, but did not expose the conspiracy. General Madanoglu joined the group after considerable hesitation. See Ipekçi and Cosar, *op. cit.*, pp. 153–60, 179, 213–15.

94. Lieuwen, *Arms and Politics in Latin America*, pp. 126–30; see also Johnson, *The Military and Society in Latin America*, p. 151; Halpern, *The Politics of Social Change in the Middle East and North Africa*, p. 262, n. 16.

95. Perlmutter, *op. cit.*, pp. 6–7.

96. See above, p. 33.

97. Weiker, *The Turkish Revolution, 1960–1961*, p. 89.

98. *Ibid.*

99. *Ibid.*, p. 156.

100. Karpat, "Recent Political Developments in Turkey and Their Social Background," p. 305; Harris, *op. cit.*, p. 176.

Books Written under the Center's Auspices

The Soviet Bloc, by Zbigniew K. Brzezinski (jointly with the Russian Research Center), 1960. Harvard University Press.

The Necessity for Choice, by Henry A. Kissinger, 1961. Harper & Bros.

Strategy and Arms Control, by Thomas C. Schelling and Morton H. Halperin, 1961. Twentieth Century Fund.

Rift and Revolt in Hungary, by Ferenc A. Váli, 1961. Harvard University Press.

United States Manufacturing Investment in Brazil, by Lincoln Gordon and Engelbert L. Grommers, 1962. Harvard Business School.

The Economy of Cyprus, by A. J. Meyer, with Simos Vassiliou (jointly with the Center for Middle Eastern Studies), 1962. Harvard University Press.

Entrepreneurs of Lebanon, by Yusif A. Sayigh (jointly with the Center for Middle Eastern Studies), 1962. Harvard University Press.

Communist China 1955-1959: Policy Documents with Analysis, with a Foreword by Robert R. Bowie and John K. Fairbank (jointly with the East Asian Research Center), 1962. Harvard University Press.

In Search of France, by Stanley Hoffmann, Charles P. Kindleberger, Laurence Wylie, Jesse R. Pitts, Jean-Baptiste Duroselle, and François Goguel, 1963. Harvard University Press.

Somali Nationalism, by Saadia Touval, 1963. Harvard University Press.

The Dilemma of Mexico's Development, by Raymond Vernon, 1963. Harvard University Press.

Limited War in the Nuclear Age, by Morton H. Halperin, 1963. John Wiley & Sons.

The Arms Debate, by Robert A. Levine, 1963. Harvard University Press.

Africans on the Land, by Montague Yudelman, 1964. Harvard University Press.

Counterinsurgency Warfare, by David Galula, 1964. Frederick A. Praeger, Inc.

People and Policy in the Middle East, by Max Weston Thornburg, 1964. W. W. Norton & Co.

Shaping the Future, by Robert R. Bowie, 1964. Columbia University Press.

Foreign Aid and Foreign Policy, by Edward S. Mason (jointly with the Council on Foreign Relations), 1964. Harper & Row.

Public Policy and Private Enterprise in Mexico, by M. S. Wionczek, D. H. Shelton, C. P. Blair, and R. Izquierdo, ed. Raymond Vernon, 1964. Harvard University Press.

How Nations Negotiate, by Fred C. Iklé, 1964. Harper & Row.

China and the Bomb, by Morton H. Halperin (jointly with the East Asian Research Center), 1965. Frederick A. Praeger, Inc.

Democracy in Germany, by Fritz Erler (Jodidi Lectures), 1965. Harvard University Press.

The Troubled Partnership, by Henry A. Kissinger (jointly with the Council on Foreign Relations), 1965. McGraw-Hill Book Co.

The Rise of Nationalism in Central Africa, by Robert I. Rotberg, 1965. Harvard University Press.

Communist China and Arms Control, by Morton H. Halperin and Dwight H. Perkins (jointly with the East Asian Research Center), 1965. Frederick A. Praeger, Inc.

Pan-Africanism and East African Integration, by Joseph S. Nye, Jr., 1965. Harvard University Press.

Problems of National Strategy, ed. Henry A. Kissinger, 1965. Frederick A. Praeger, Inc.

Deterrence before Hiroshima: The Airpower Background of Modern Strategy, by George H. Quester, 1966. John Wiley & Sons.

Containing the Arms Race, by Jeremy J. Stone, 1966. M.I.T. Press.

Germany and the Atlantic Alliance, by James L. Richardson, 1966. Harvard University Press.

Arms and Influence, by Thomas C. Schelling, 1966. Yale University Press.

Political Change in a West African State, by Martin L. Kilson, 1966. Harvard University Press.

Planning without Facts, by Wolfgang Stolper, 1966. Harvard University Press.